The French Foreign Legion

The French Foreig

egion

ames Wellard

dré Deutsch

This book was designed and produced by
George Rainbird Limited,
Marble Arch House, 44 Edgware Road,
London, W2,
for André Deutsch Limited
105 Great Russell Street
London WC1B 3LJ

Picture Research by: Felicity Luard
Designer: Judith Allan
Maps by: Tom Stalker-Miller
Indexer: Myra Clark

First published 1974
© James Wellard 1974

Filmset in Monophoto Plantin by
BAS Printers Limited, Wallop, Hampshire

Printed and bound by
Cox & Wyman Limited, Fakenham, Norfolk

Colour plates printed by Alabaster Passmore

ISBN: 0 233 96560 2

Printed in Great Britain

Contents

Foreword

In the course of its one hundred and forty-three years of existence, the
Foreign Legion has been the subject of a great deal of romantic fiction
on the one hand and exaggerated abuse on the other. English-speaking
readers tend to base their knowledge of the Legion on the kind of novel
which originated with a work published in 1867 called *Under Two Flags*
by Marie Louise de la Ramée, *alias* Ouida. This writer, in fact, can be
said to have created the stereotype of the legionnaire as a misunderstood
gentleman (her legionnaire was an officer in the Guards who sought
solace from his misfortunes in the deserts of North Africa). The writer
P. C. Wren brought the image up to date in his Beau Geste novels of the
1920s. After that came a spate of memoirs by ex-legionnaires, many of
them deserters, writing between 1920 and 1939 when the Legion,
together with the French government, was under attack because of the
Moroccan War. But in the end, the romantic myth created by Ouida
and her successors continued to be the accepted idea of the Legion.

A student of the subject today finds that both the romance and the
abuse are of little value in assessing the significance of this unique corps,
since they miss the point of its story. The point is that the Legion is not
simply a haphazard collection of misunderstood or lovelorn adventurers
or, for that matter, of fugitives from justice, but that it has played an
integral part in European history, particularly the history of the French
Empire, and it can be studied in that light. The present writer has
attempted to do this, believing that such an appraisal is the best way to
tell the story in a reasonably objective manner, without getting too
involved in either the panegyrics of those who loved the Legion or the
detractions of those who hated it.

In researching and writing this brief history of the Legion, I received
help and advice from many sources. I would like to thank the officers
and legionnaires who received me at headquarters in Aubagne and
Puyloubier. Special thanks are due to the President and Honorary
Secretary of the Foreign Legion Association of Great Britain, Maurice
Pomerand and John Yeowell; and to all those *anciens combattants* who
took the trouble to write to me and express their views. I have quoted
extracts from their letters in the following pages, but would again like

to thank all of them for their generous response to my requests for help and information.

My thanks, too, go to previous Legion historians whose works are listed in the bibliography, and bibliographical notes where appropriate; and to the Superintendent and staff of the Reading Room of the British Museum who made these invaluable sources available.

Finally this volume has been made possible by the expert counsel and cooperation of the producer George Rainbird Ltd, whose director David Herbert, the house editor Erica Hunningher, the picture researcher Felicity Luard, the designer Judith Allan and the cartographer Tom Stalker-Miller have worked with me from the beginning.

The Legion, Hollywood thirties style. Gary Cooper, Ray Milland, and Robert Preston in *Beau Geste*; (below) Gary Cooper and Marlene Dietrich in *Morocco*.

Portrait of a Legionnaire

Volunteers came from all over the world, fugitives running away from the police, from their enemies, their families, even from themselves.

The place they were bound for was the main reception centre of the Foreign Legion inside the Fort St Jean which used to guard the Old Harbour of Marseilles until it was bombed in the Second World War. The majority of those who passed through the gateway into the grim fortress had few illusions about what was in store for them, for the Foreign Legion has never been presented in the same romantic light to Continental Europeans as it has to readers of English fiction. And perhaps the false picture thus given to Anglo-Saxon volunteers explains why the most bitter indictments of the Legion have, for the most part, been written by British or American deserters who discovered what life was really like inside the training camps and desert forts of Africa.

Yet the Legion cannot be accused of romanticizing itself. On the contrary, it has always preferred to remain reticent about its activities, for it has been aware from the beginning that both the general public and the military in France have regarded the corps with a certain suspicion.[1] Its attitude towards the outside world, in fact, has always been one of indifference, as though it were a law unto itself. It is certainly a separate world into which no one who is not an inhabitant can really enter.

Once the corps had proved by its deeds that it was the most valuable fighting unit in the French army, it no longer needed to recruit volunteers from the fugitives of society, whether these were criminals on the run or gentlemen escaping from their wives or their debts. By 1890, when the English journalist George Manington joined the Legion, the unit had ceased to be a refuge for misfits and was, to the contrary, in a position to discourage 'respectable' young men attracted to the service because of their adventurous spirit, as was Manington himself. Manington, who applied at a recruiting station in Paris in 1890, records this conversation with the French major who interviewed him:

A legionnaire stands in front of the recruiting station at Fort St Jean, on the western side of the old port at Marseilles.

Service uniforms of nineteenth-century legionnaires: (*left to right*) rifleman
(1848); grenadier (Algeria 1848); infantryman (Mexico 1861); legionnaire
(1870).

'Since when have you decided to enlist in one of the Régiments Etrangers?'
  'Oh! Since yesterday.'
  He smiled, and then said, to my astonishment and anger:
'*Eh bien!* You are a fool, my friend. Ah! that hurts you, doesn't it? Sure
proof that stern discipline would not suit you . . . The Legion – why, you
don't know what it is. Well, I will tell you – hard work – hard knocks –
hard discipline, and no thanks. And how does it end? Your throat cut by
some thieving Arab if you have luck: if not, wounded, and then his woman
makes sausagemeat of you . . . You look like a gentleman – you are one,
I'm sure. Your family, too! Think of them – such a sudden decision. And
all for some trifling *bêtise*, *sans doute*. A petticoat, I'll swear – a faithless
sweetheart. Pish! There are a thousand others who would be delighted to
console you. No! No! A good dinner, the *Moulin Rouge*, and tomorrow
you will be cured.'[2]

Régiments Étrangers (Légion Etrangève) 1914.

Tenue de Ville   Tenue de Compagne   Tenue d'Ordinaire   Tenue du Tonki
                        (Algérie)

Legion uniforms of the early twentieth century: (*left to right*) dress uniform;
battle dress (Algeria); service uniform (1914); service uniform (Tonkin).

Such, then, was the bored attitude of the recruiting officers towards
the scores of seekers after glamour who stood before their desks, every
day of the year, in Paris and Marseilles, the main centres of recruitment.
At Marseilles, in the hall of Fort St Jean, the Legion 'law' was certainly
made crystal clear, for the inscription on the wall read:

> VOUS ETES SOLDATS POUR MOURIR,
> ET JE VOUS ENVOIE LA OU L'ON MEURT.

It could hardly be more uncompromising than that – a legionnaire was
a soldier in order to die, and he must expect to be used for exactly that
purpose. So, at any rate, said General François Oscar de Négrier during
the 1883–91 campaign in Indo-China; and in this case, the words meant
precisely what they said. The casualties suffered by the Legion proved it.

But perhaps even more typical of service in the Legion than the acceptance of death on the battlefield was what was called the *règlement*: that is, the conditions of discipline and training which, from the outset, were enforced with a severity which many of those who had experienced it described as sheer sadism. The ordeal began as soon as a volunteer had passed through the gates of headquarters at Sidi-bel-Abbès. Once issued with his heavy and ill-fitting uniform, the recruit was mustered on to the parade ground and inducted by veteran non-commissioned officers into the routine of drill and the dreaded route-marches. Marching, in fact, very early in the Legion's history had become the foundation of training and seems to have been copied from the Roman infantry's ability to march twenty miles a day, or twenty-five at an accelerated rate. The foreign legionnaire was expected to do more – to march up to thirty miles, if need be, loaded down with his huge knapsack, rifle, bayonet, pick or shovel, 300 rounds of ammunition, and wood for his fire – all this in full uniform, including an army greatcoat. Every man marched or was driven along by the sergeants; or, if he could not get to his feet, he was dragged behind the mule cart which followed the column. The justification for this form of torture was the Legion slogan, *March or die*, a precept originating from the early campaigns in the Sahara where a man could not hope to survive unless he kept his place in the column. And so men who had seldom walked as much as five miles at a time in their lives, men who were physically unfit, men who were still not acclimatized to the African heat, men who were suffering from dysentery or heat exhaustion, all were forced on their first day of real training to set off on a long march in full woollen uniform and carrying full kit. Staggering along, they were ordered from time to time to sing, since singing on the march was another feature of the *règlement*.

But by the time George Manington joined the Legion in 1890, this part of the training was less rigorous, for he reports that the first real route-march was twelve and a half miles, the recruit carrying only his rifle and side-arms. The distance was gradually increased until the soldier marched twenty-eight miles a day 'with ease', carrying a total weight of fifty pounds. We see that the accounts of the famous Legion marching are often completely contradictory, the detractors, on the one hand, insisting that the exercise was utterly sadistic, the apologists, like Manington, maintaining that the men themselves were 'very proud of their capabilities in this respect'.[3]

But as in all accounts of the soldier's life, the overall impression varies with the writer's point of view. There were those ex-legionnaires who

Captain Aage, the Danish prince who served with the Legion in
Morocco, personified the high ideals of a Legion officer.

hated the corps with an ill-concealed loathing, just as there were others
who loved and extolled it. As one might expect, the former were almost
without exception deserters who had made their plans to desert from
the moment they had put on the uniform. The apologists were usually
enlisted men who completed their service honourably; in particular,
officers whose experiences of Legion life have, admittedly, little in
common with those of the private soldier. So we find an officer like
Captain Aage, a Danish prince, who joined the Legion in 1922 and
served as a junior officer throughout the Moroccan campaign, extolling
the corps without reservation in his book, *My Life in the Foreign Legion*.[4]
Actually Prince Aage's book is a hymn in praise of the romance of war,
for the Dane is honest enough not to try to disguise his love of the
military life or the fact that he found in the Legion an escape from the
tame existence of peace-time soldiering. Indeed, practically every
account written by ex-officers confirms Prince Aage's view, though only
rarely does one come across similar sentiments in the writings of the
ordinary soldiers. The diary of the American poet Alan Seeger is to this
extent the more surprising.

Alan Seeger (1888–1916) enlisted in the Foreign Legion in 1914 and
was in the front lines for almost two years before dying of his wounds
in a shell-hole outside the village of Belloy-en-Santerre. The *Croix de
Guerre* and the *Médaille Militaire* were conferred upon him post-
humously, but he will be remembered more for the poems he wrote in
the trenches where, indeed, he wrote his own epitaph:

> I have a rendezvous with Death
> At some disputed barricade,
> When Spring comes back with rustling shade
> And apple-blossoms fill the air –
> I have a rendezvous with Death. . . .[5]

It was, then, unusually romantic individuals like a Danish prince and
an American poet who gave the Legion the image which was to be
exploited in the fiction and films of the twenties and thirties. But long
before the novelists had invented the *beau geste* theme, the Legion had
attracted volunteers distinguished by their birth, or wealth, or eccen-
tricities. One of the very earliest accounts of this unique trait is
given by Count Pierre de Castellane, a heroic figure of nineteenth-
century French military history, who found such a collection of unusual men on his visit in 1844 to the Legion fort of Khemis sixty miles
east of Algiers in the country of the Kabyles. De Castellane describes
the type of outpost which was to become the classic redoubt of the
Legion for the next hundred years. It consisted of a mud-brick fort
with a look-out tower at each corner, like many a similar outpost still to
be seen today half-covered with sand deep in the Sahara desert. There
were 300 men on garrison duty in this fort of Khemis. They slept in
hammocks in barrack rooms inside the walls. Three rooms were reserved
for their officers. In the centre of the courtyard stood the base of a
Roman column, on which someone had placed a sundial. The only
other ornament of the fort was a large tree under which the officers
gathered in the evenings to exchange news and gossip while sipping
absinthe. Here de Castellane met the son of a privy councillor to the
Austrian Emperor Francis II, the nephew of a Cardinal, the son of a
German banker, and Lieutenant Thomas Lansdowne Parr Moore,
eldest son of the Irish poet and godson of Lord Byron. We see in the
French count's description of Lieutenant Moore the origin of the
myth of the broken-hearted lover – a myth that most commentators
who had actually served in the Legion deny, maintaining, to the contrary, that men volunteered not because they loved but because they

hated a certain woman. But of Lieutenant Thomas Moore, the French count writes:

His manners were particularly gentlemanly, and his glossy black hair, clear complexion, straight nose, and liquid brilliant eye, full of intelligence, gave everyone at once a strong impression in his favour. A slight accent betrayed the Irishman . . . Moore often took the portrait of a beautiful woman from his bosom and gazed earnestly upon it when he thought himself unobserved. . . .[6]

'Alas!' says de Castellane, 'though his eyes sparkled when he spoke of returning home, I heard with terror the dry cough which his excitement caused and noted the red spots on his cheeks.' In fact, Thomas Moore was to die a few months later somewhere in Algeria. He was thirty-three years old and, as far as we know, the first Briton to serve in the Foreign Legion.

In stark contrast to these romantic or poetic descriptions of life in the Legion are the accounts of the rank and file who found the system so intolerable that they bent all their energies to escaping, even though well aware that desertion was the one crime which the Legion would never countenance. Those who did manage to get away wrote their 'revelations' under such titles as *Hell in the Foreign Legion, Slaves of Morocco, Hell Hounds of France, Legion of the Lost, Legion of the Damned,* and so forth. Many of these hostile accounts reiterate the charge that the average legionnaire was so brutalized that his only pleasures were wine and sex. A German deserter, Ernst Löhndorff, who tells us he joined the Legion for reasons of 'unemployment, desire for warmth, bread, and a wife', speaks of the 'God Alcohol, the Lord of the Legion, the Booze that drags us all down'.[7] Drunkenness, in short, was so endemic that normal social relations were almost impossible, both within and without the Legion.

In consequence the hostility shown towards the Legion by the citizens of towns where the regiments were stationed is understandable, since, when off duty, the soldiers were liable to rob, abuse, and beat up the owners of cafés, restaurants, and wine-shops, as well as any innocent bystanders who happened to get involved in their drunken brawls. The result was the further isolation of the legionnaires who sank deeper and deeper into desperation. This process is well described by an Anglo-Irish deserter, Michael Donovan, in his book, *March or Die!*

Every man who joins the Legion does so in ignorance of what awaits him. If the real conditions of Legion life were known, the Legion as such would soon cease to exist, for it would not get a single recruit. *Men become beasts before they have worn the uniform for a year.*

The cramped conditions and lack of privacy of a Legion dormitory at Sidi-bel-Abbès required every legionnaire to conform to the system, even to placing his boots at a precise spot under his bed.

Three months after I joined, I found myself laughing at the expressions on the face of a prisoner who had been stripped naked and tied by his thumbs to a wall with his toes barely touching the ground . . . I have seen other prisoners go mad when serving the same sentence.[8]

One could repeat *ad nauseam* specific examples of brutality as reported by ex-legionnaires of every nationality, examples of tortures inflicted on them and even worse cruelties dealt out to their enemies. But while admitting – as all fair commentators must – that the *règlement* of the Legion was harsh, and often unnecessarily so, one must try to balance the accounts of the detractors on the one side and the apologists on the other. It is noticeable, for instance, that every writer who hates and condemns the Legion also despises and decries his fellow-legionnaires; and since, in the old days, many of them were murderers, thieves, cut-throats, *et cetera*, it is evident that they could not be turned into disciplined soldiers by the training methods one would employ with a troop of boy scouts. The majority of them were, without doubt, desperate or unhappy to the point of paranoia, and this is nowhere better illustrated than in an incident described by Michael Donovan. He tells us that 'a cold rage swept over me', and he hit another legionnaire on the chin, 'completely forgetting that I had a heavy steel bolt in my hand'. His blow started a chain reaction throughout the room, for, in a few moments,

> ... screams and curses filled the air, and I leapt onto the table and swung out with my rifle at anyone who approached. In one corner of the room I saw half-a-dozen men stabbing at one another with their bayonets, while here and there a man already lay senseless on the floor in a pool of blood.[9]

Donovan paints the picture of a roomful of homicidal maniacs, and one is not altogether surprised to learn that the sergeant responsible for quelling this riot did so by ordering a machine-gunner to fire at the doors and windows of the barracks. The fighting inside stopped at once.

All the other books by deserters recount similar atrocities, leaving the reader with the impression of a drunken, foul-mouthed, and hopeless company of men without a glimmer of dignity, let alone romance. Even the descriptions of the desert forts, the very mainspring of Hollywood's versions of the Foreign Legion, reveal that life in these outposts was a living death. If anything, the *cafard* (that state of despair brought on by hopelessness, literally the 'black beetle') was worse in the forts than it was in the barracks of the large towns. It turned the men into 'lunatics and bleating idiots – the majority spiritually degenerated with neither will nor energy; the rest teeth-gnashing, eye-rolling victims of frenzy', according to the German deserter, Ernst Löhndorff. Here he is describing a legion outpost on the northern fringe of the vast Algerian sand sea called the Grand Erg Occidental.

> Fort Jonnart with its high walls, watch-tower, seven date palms, and well. Here a rebellious legionnaire is taken outside the fort, stripped, and buried naked up to the neck. Within half-an-hour all spirit of rebellion has gone out of him. So was the spirit of the Englishman A. R. Cooper broken by his period in the dreaded Penal Battalion where he was confined for fifteen days in a hole like a grave especially dug in the ground and then 'given a taste of the crapaudin' which meant having his wrists and ankles tied together behind his back.[10]

What conclusions, then, are we to draw concerning the Legion and its *règlement*? And what kind of man is the legionnaire?

The hard core of the regiments has always been and continues to be the Germans and South Europeans. These men, the Germans in particular, enlist because they *want* to make war and so are prepared to accept the severe and rigid discipline as a fact of the mercenary's life.

Others accept it because they like to be led. But the Anglo-Saxons, according to the French, find it difficult to fit into a system whose language (or indeed, languages), routine, and discipline are completely unfamiliar to them, which may explain why so many books condemning the Legion have been written by English or American deserters.

How reliable are such books? According to the English legionnaire, ex-sergeant A. R. Cooper, 'I have found only two books in which the whole truth was told, one by Prince Haag [*sic*] of Denmark, the other by Major Pechkoff [*sic*], the adopted son of Maxim Gorki.'[11] Both Aage and Pechkov speak as admitted apologists for the French colonial system and its wars, writing about battles which belonged to the last of the nineteenth-century campaigns which were won by the courage, discipline, and endurance of the individual soldier. Further, both Prince Aage's and Major Pechkov's diaries are imbued with the spirit of the chivalric or knightly code whereby a soldier and particularly an officer, conducted himself like a gentleman. In one engagement, Major Pechkov stayed with his men until they noticed that he was bleeding from a wound and insisted on lifting him from his horse. (Incidentally, having only one arm, Pechkov used to mount by holding the reins between his teeth and springing into the saddle with the help of his remaining hand.) Admired and even loved by his soldiers, the Russian officer understood the very soul of the Legion and so could write these simple words which sum up the deepest feelings of the true legionnaire:

> The flag is being raised over the post, slowly rising above the white walls and taken by the burning breeze into the blue sky. Every man who is outside of the barracks in the post, even all the natives who are living in the annex, when they hear the bugle and see the flag rising, stop and stand motionless. Perfect silence reigns.
>
> I like this primitive life. I feel so strong and gay. I feel in communion with my men.[12]

Prince Aage, too, emphasizes that special quality which helps to give the Legion its *mystique*, of which we have an intimation in this description of a fellow-officer:

> Major M— makes it a point never to be armed. He claims that, in the first place, an officer should set an example rather than fight; and that, in the second, the weight of a revolver causes one's belt to sag and this spoils the set of one's tunic.[13]

Such eccentricity was not, in fact, unusual among the Legion's officers. General Paul Rollet, whose bravery and love of the corps earned him the title of *père de la Légion*, always went into battle unarmed; yet he ended his active military career as one of the most decorated soldiers in the French army.

But in the final analysis, if the observer wishes to get a fair picture of the Legion and the legionnaires, he must take into account deeds as well as words. Whereas the *règlement* and its methods are, and always will be, highly controversial, there can be no argument about its achievements. The Company Standards emblazoned with battle honours and the motto 'Honour and Fidelity' are symbolic of those achievements.

We begin at the beginning, which is both curious and unexpected.

Legion standard of the First Regiment (1855–6): the motto on the reverse *Valeur et Discipline*.

Louis-Philippe, Roi des Français,

À tous présens et à venir, Salut.

Les Chambres ont adopté, Nous avons ordonné
et ordonnons ce qui suit :

Article 1.er

Il pourra être formé dans l'intérieur du Royaume, une
légion d'étrangers; mais elle ne pourra être employée que hors
du territoire continental du Royaume.

Article 2.

Les généraux en chef commandant les pays occupés par les
armées françaises, hors du territoire continental, pourront être
autorisés à former des corps militaires composés d'indigènes et d'étrangers.

Article 3.

Les dépenses de ces divers corps forment un article séparé au Budget de la guerre.

La présente loi, discutée, délibérée et adoptée par la chambre des Pairs
et par celle des Députés et sanctionnée par nous ce jourd'hui, sera exécutée
comme loi de l'État.

Donnons en mandement à nos Cours et Tribunaux, Préfets, Corps
administratifs et tous autres, que les présentes ils gardent et maintiennent,
fassent garder, observer et maintenir, et, pour les rendre plus notoires à tous,
ils les fassent publier et enregistrer partout où besoin sera, et, afin que ce soit
chose ferme et stable à toujours, Nous y avons fait mettre Notre Sceau.

Donné à Paris, au Palais Royal le Neuf Mars,
mil huit cent trente-un.

Louis Philippe

Par le Roi,

Le Ministre secrétaire d'État de la Guerre,
Mal. Duc de Dalmatie

Vu et Scellé du Grand Sceau :
Le Ministre Secrétaire d'État au Département
de la Marine et des Colonies, remplissant par
intérim les fonctions de Garde des Sceaux,
Ministre de la Justice

V. Dupont

The Origin of the Foreign Legion

From the Equator to the Arctic circle, in almost every continent and major war of the last 143 years, the Foreign Legion has fought and legionnaires have died in such a dramatic manner that the corps has become a legend. More, it has created a special *mystique* of its own, best summed up by its own terse phrase: *La Légion est la Légion*. This *mystique* is partly based on its long list of victories on battlefields as far apart as Indo-China and Central America, and perhaps even more on its heroic defeats, for this band of rather despised mercenaries could be expected to die to the last man, and sometimes did, in wars of the late nineteenth century and up to the second half of the twentieth century. Thus the entire First Parachute Battalion of the Legion was wiped out in 1950 at Cao Bang in Vietnam and, re-formed, was wiped out again several months later at Dien Bien Phu. The Legion, in other words, was regarded as expendable, and the legionnaires very early in their history learnt to think of themselves accordingly. This attitude, too, contributed greatly to the legend which made this body of men famous the world over in books and films, sometimes as the romantic figures of fiction, sometimes as the 'Legion of the Damned', sometimes as the embodiment of heroism.

Yet the origins of the Legion were far from romantic: this special unit of the French army, this *'légion composée d'étrangers'*, was formed as a political expedient in 1831, by order of the French king, Louis Philippe. As far as the High Command was concerned, the king's proposal for coping with a collection of political refugees, revolutionaries, and fugitives was a military joke. Louis Philippe thought otherwise. He had just come to the throne after a rebellion which ousted his predecessor, the hated Bourbon, Charles X, and the new monarch was, with reason, apprehensive about his own security. He was well aware that revolutions, civil wars, and the fall of kings were typical of the whole of

The historic charter of Louis Philippe founding 'a Legion composed of foreigners'. It stipulated that such a Legion should be employed only outside continental France; but by 1870, thirty-nine years after the decree was signed, the Legion was fighting in the streets of Paris.

Europe in the first half of the nineteenth century. There had been uprisings in Poland, Germany, Belgium, Italy, Spain, and Portugal; and
one result of the continuous disturbances was a flood of political refugees,
army deserters, and revolutionaries fleeing from their homelands. Louis
Philippe was not happy about these hordes of exiles, particularly as
France was now engaged in a war in North Africa which precluded the
use of the army from keeping the peace at home. The idea, therefore,
was to round up as many of these exiles as possible and to ship them
abroad. But how was this to be done without sowing the seeds of yet
another revolution?

The solution was proposed by a mysterious Belgian adventurer called
Lacroix, self-styled 'Baron Böegard' and self-created lieutenant-
general. Lacroix had, in fact, already assembled a band of foreigners
whom he proposed to send to Algeria to fight with the French army or to
settle as colonists. According to contemporary reports they were an
assortment of unemployed workers, professional revolutionaries, lonely
old men, deserters, and vagabonds, who were formed into companies
commanded by an officer of their own election. 'The most curious is a
tailor,' writes Captain Blanc of the French army. 'He made himself
commanding officer by virtue of his services to the local community,
and he brought certificates signed by the local shopkeepers to prove it.'[1]
But Lacroix's suggestion that unwanted foreigners without means of
subsistence should be drafted into a 'legion' and shipped forthwith to
Africa was readily accepted by the French king who, on 9 and 10 of
March 1831, issued a decree authorizing the formation of *une légion
composée d'étrangers*. The royal order stipulated that:

1. Such a legion should only be employed outside the frontiers of continental France.
2. All applicants should be between the ages of 18 and 40 and not less than
   5ft in height.
3. All applicants should be furnished with a birth certificate, a testimonial
   of good conduct, and a document from a military authority stating that
   they had the necessary requirements for making a good soldier.
4. The uniform of the legion should be blue, the piping red, and the
   trousers of the same colour.[2]

Once the royal decree had become law, recruiting stations were set up
in the provinces, and volunteers were encouraged to come forward and
sign on with the promise of French citizenship at the end of their service.
It is very unlikely that the non-commissioned officers who interviewed
the volunteers paid much attention to the letter of the law, certainly not

to the stipulation requiring the applicant to produce a certificate of good conduct. The proof that practically any foreigner who was not lame, halt, or blind was accepted soon became evident when the first detachment of this Foreign Legion landed in Algiers. An eyewitness who watched them come ashore from the troop ship likened them to a circus. Their ages, he said, ranged from sixteen to sixty, and they were dressed in such an assortment of uniforms that the army must have ransacked all the military museums of France to fit them out – some in uniforms of the 1789 National Guard, others in those of the Imperial Guard, the Royal Guard, the Swiss Guard, the infantry, cavalry, artillery, *et cetera.* They marched ashore with their new flag – a cock rampant with its talon on a globe marked FRANCE – singing a popular song of the day,

Legionnaires of the First Regiment halt by the road for a makeshift meal, watched by their former enemies the Kabyles.

La Parisienne. Such was the vanguard of a force that was to become the most famous battle group in history.

A few months later another battalion landed in North Africa, but their appearance on the scene was not so amusing. The first day these legionnaires arrived, thirty-five of them deserted. On the second day an entire company got drunk and attacked their officers. Subsequently the

entire battalion had to be rounded up and incarcerated in army compounds or local jails. Two of the ringleaders were court-martialled and shot.

Obviously the authorities were not going to tolerate this sort of behaviour in the midst of a war, and so the toughest veterans of the old Prussian and Swiss regiments, who had served as the royal guards of the French kings, were now brought in to enforce discipline and restore order. There were seven battalions to cope with, three of them consisting of German political refugees and army deserters; one battalion of Spaniards; one of Italians, Sicilians, and Sardinians; one of Belgians and Dutch; and one of Poles. These troops were quickly despatched to outposts of the newly-conquered territory in Algeria and put to work building roads and blockhouses behind the front lines. Untrained and untried, these legionnaires deserted by the dozen, 'seduced', according to a contemporary report, 'by Arab promises of money and women'. The reasons for these continual desertions were more probably those that have always applied in the long history of the Legion: many men had only joined in order to get overseas and then disappear into the

(_above_) Algiers before the French occupation in 1830. (_opposite_) Louis Philippe, king of the French (1830–48), founded the Foreign Legion by royal decree in 1831, as a means of ridding France of the refugees and revolutionaries threatening his régime.

unknown, while still others found that they could not endure the privations, boredom, and brutality of an inhumane system.

The number of desertions in the early days of the Legion was, then, typical of its future history. So, too, was the first engagement in which a small detachment of legionnaires was involved a few weeks after their arrival in Algeria. On this occasion, twenty-seven out of twenty-eight

of them, along with their Swiss officer, Lieutenant Cham, were wiped out by the Arabs (nineteenth-century French military historians often called the Algerians 'Arabs') after having been abandoned by the regular army and left to defend a position just outside Algiers. All of the dead were mutilated by having their genitals excised, and this, too, became an accepted hazard of the North African campaign. But even though it is clear that the twenty-seven legionnaires died because they were outnumbered, they were none the less paid the usual lip homage accorded to those who lost their lives 'In the service of France'. The commander of the French army in North Africa, General Camille-Alphonse Trezel, publicly announced that 'the soldiers of the Foreign Legion showed great bravery in battle, as they show a particular aptitude for undergoing fatigue, heat, and privations without appearing to suffer'.

Even more important for the future of the corps, it had quickly become apparent to the French High Command that the battalions of foreigners, who had occasioned such mirth or derision when they first appeared on the scene, could be fashioned into an exceptionally valuable weapon, once the old soldiers – officers and sergeants from the regular

(*opposite*) Until the French army offered rewards for information leading to the capture of deserters, a legionnaire could go to an 'agency' in the native quarter of Algiers, sell his uniform, and quietly 'disappear'.

army – had disciplined and trained them. The argument was that these stateless men had, in effect, sold themselves as mercenaries and could therefore be legitimately used for the most dangerous assignments.

The battle flags tell something of the Legion's heroic story, of frontal assaults on the enemy's fortified positions – in North Africa, Mexico, the Crimea, Indo-China, Flanders, and elsewhere; but they do not reveal the psychology of the men who appear to have died so readily and in such numbers. We must look for the explanation of this phenomenon in motives quite different from those that enabled the Spartans to die at Thermopylae. For it was not necessarily patriotism, or a love of France, or even allegiance to the French army that animated the foreign legionnaires: it was the relentless training and discipline that made these men such superb soldiers. And again, the reason for this is found in the origins of the Legion, particularly in the determination of the first commanders to crush all attempts at desertion, drunkenness, and unmilitary conduct. They sometimes did so by employing the type of non-commissioned officer who 'broke' men as some trainers break horses and mules – by sheer brutality.

We can hardly be surprised, therefore, that the legionnaires differed from other professional soldiers in their indifference to their own as well as their opponents' sufferings; for the nature of their conditioning and the severity of their *règlement* inevitably set them apart from their fellows. It was, indeed, this sense of isolation which impelled numbers of them to desert at all costs and, failing escape, to commit suicide. For these desperate men, the Legion really was a Legion of the Damned. Given this attitude of either complete resignation or utter hopelessness, it is easier to understand why they were so often used in desperate situations, why they accepted impossible assignments, and why they died in such numbers. The French military hero, Count Georges Henri Marie Anne Victor de Villebois-Mareuil, sums up that attitude in his description of a legionnaire in the trenches before Sevastopol. He writes:

> He is standing up, though he would be wiser to duck down for safety.
> But it is a legionnaire's nature to stand upright in the face of danger . . .
> His old soldier's face is thoughtful, but at the same time hardened by firm
> resolution. One feels that he is impervious to the intense cold, as he is to
> everything but the enemy, while he devotes himself body and soul to his
> single goal in life – to die bravely at his post. Looking at him, one is sure
> that nothing will move him from that resolve.[3]

Behind this fustian, some of which is plainly nonsensical (the soldier's alleged refusal to take cover, for example), lies a tribute to the legionnaire's unquestioned courage. But it will be seen that courage of this kind stems from the fact that men without a country, without a family, without a career, or any place in normal society have nothing to lose even on the battlefield. This attitude is, then, the true secret of that *mystique* which differentiates the corps from other élite regiments. For once a volunteer had passed through the portals of the depot at Sidi-bel-Abbès, the former headquarters of the Legion in Algeria, he had no other home or homeland. Nationality, social status, and personal relations were of no concern to the Legion. They belonged to a man's past, like his crimes if he had committed them, or his misfortunes and his private miseries. In this knowledge men came from all over the world to find a home at Sidi, so that by the end of the nineteenth century, the First Regiment of the Legion included twenty-six different nationalities, among them twenty-nine Americans, twenty-one British, twenty-nine Turks, nine Greeks, one Senegalese, and a man described simply as 'a Hindu'.[1]

From this conglomeration of nations and races emerged the prototype of the legionnaire.

Berbers were forced to flee with their livestock, abandoning their homes, when the French made sudden raids on their villages.

The French in Africa

The French first occupied the coastal cities and plains in their gradual conquest of Algeria. Their principal enemies were the terrain and climate, and their reliance on large armies. Later, they realized the desert could only be conquered by small mobile forces, like the Camel Corps, the *Chasseurs d'Afrique*, the *Spahis*, and the Legion's Mounted Companies. And as the vanguard fought its way from oasis to oasis, the Legion built and manned strategic forts, made tracks across the wasteland, and sent patrols against desert raiders. The invasion lasted for over a hundred years and finally brought France an African Empire comprising 3,866,950 square miles of territory.

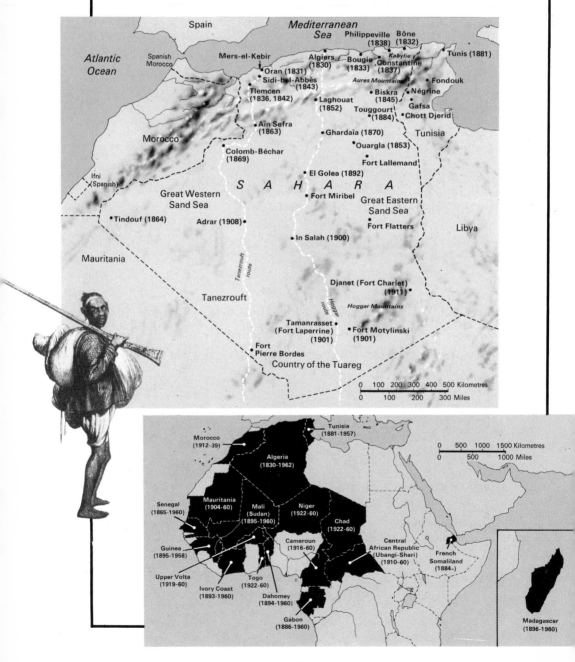

Spain

Mediterranean Sea

Atlantic Ocean

Spanish Morocco

Mers-el-Kebir

Philippeville (1838)   Bône (1832)

Tunis (1881)

Algiers (1830)   Bougie (1833)   Constantine (1837)   Kabylie

Oran (1831)
Sidi-bel-Abbès (1843)

Fondouk

Tlemcen (1836, 1842)

Aures Mountains

Laghouat (1852)

Biskra (1845)   Négrine

Touggourt (1884)   Gafsa

Chott Djerid

Morocco

Aïn Sefra (1863)

Colomb-Béchar (1869)

Ghardaïa (1870)

Ouargla (1853)

Fort Lallemand

Tunisia

Ifni (Spanish)

El Golea (1892)

S A H A R A

Great Western Sand Sea

Fort Miribel

Great Eastern Sand Sea

Tindouf (1864)

Adrar (1908)

Fort Flatters

Libya

Mauritania

In Salah (1900)

Tanezrouft route

Tanezrouft

Djanet (Fort Charlet) (1911)

Hoggar route

Hoggar Mountains

Tamanrasset (Fort Laperrine) (1901)

Fort Motylinski (1901)

Fort Pierre Bordes

Country of the Tuareg

0   100   200   300   400   500 Kilometres
0   100   200   300 Miles

Morocco (1912-39)

Tunisia (1881-1957)

0   500   1000   1500 Kilometres
0   500   1000 Miles

Algeria (1830-1962)

Senegal (1865-1960)

Mauritania (1904-60)

Mali (Sudan) (1895-1960)

Niger (1922-60)

Chad (1922-60)

Cameroun (1916-60)

Central African Republic (Ubangi-Shari) (1910-60)

French Somaliland (1884-)

Guinea (1895-1958)

Upper Volta (1919-60)

Ivory Coast (1893-1960)

Togo (1922-60)

Dahomey (1894-1960)

Gabon (1886-1960)

Madagascar (1896-1960)

The First African Campaigns 1835-63

It is said that there is scarcely a mountain, ravine, valley or oasis, from the shores of the North African coast to the banks of the Niger River, where the bodies of the legionnaires do not lie, some with little monuments which one can still see, some without any grave at all. It would take several volumes to recount in detail all the engagements, major and minor, which the Legion fought in the conquest of the four million square miles which constituted the French African empire.

Certainly North Africa was the cradle of the Legion, and it was here in this beautiful yet savage territory of eroded mountains and vast sand seas that the corps rose to greatness – not only as a military unit, but as a force that built roads, bridges, forts, and even towns. In these achievements the French Foreign Legion can be compared with the Roman Third Augusta Legion which kept the peace and built up the civilization of North Africa for 400 years.[1]

And like the Third Augusta, which built its own headquarters at Lambessa and its own city of Timgad in eastern Algeria, so the Foreign Legion founded the headquarters and city of Sidi-bel-Abbès in western Algeria. When the Legion chose this site in 1843, Sidi consisted of nothing but the shrine of a local holy man. When the corps left in 1962, it was a city of 105,000 people, nearly all of it laid out and built by Legion architects and engineers. Throughout Algeria, as the army pushed southwards, the Legion built roads and forts almost exactly as the Third Augusta had done 1,600 years before them; and the end results were the same as those following the Roman conquest of Numidia: a region of nomadic tribes was transformed into a prosperous and civilized nation.

The price that had to be paid in human lives, both of the conquerors and the conquered, was, however, enormous, and herein lies one of the main differences between the operations of the Roman army in North Africa and those of the French. The Romans, for instance, employed only one legion of 10,000 men to conquer and police the whole of North Africa, from Libya in the east to Morocco in the west. In October 1837 the French mustered 10,000 men for the attack on the Algerian city of Constantine alone. This enormous force, under General Damrémont and his chief-of-staff Perregaux, is shown in contemporary paintings and prints with the various battalions, including a newly-formed battalion of the Foreign Legion, marching shoulder to shoulder up to the walls of the city, every man clad in a heavy woollen uniform, though the temperature was in the nineties. In the meantime, the French cannon were trying to breach the walls, but intelligence seems to have been so poor that Damrémont and Perregaux had no idea of the weight and accuracy of the enemy's artillery, with the result that the former was killed by a shell and the latter severely wounded before the actual siege had begun. In short, the commander of the army and his chief-of-staff exposed themselves to risks which modern strategists would consider wholly unjustified.

Such tactics, however, were to become characteristic of the Legion. During the battle for Constantine, for instance, the same tactics were employed – the storming of barricades, the rushing through streets, the waving of flags and blowing of bugles, the charges led by officers waving their swords – all seemed to have been performed in true Hollywood epic style. So a company of the Legion, led by Captain Edouard Joseph Saint-Arnaud, later to become a Marshal of France, stormed through a barricade, raced along a street in the face of point-blank fire and were duly 'mown down' as their captain rallied them with the cry that was to become the watchword of the Legion, '*A moi la Légion!*' Still, Constantine was taken; and it is not surprising that the public and politicians back home declared that it was *magnifique*, despite the casualties.

And so the Battle of Constantine set the pattern for the Legion's role in the many wars to come. Frontal assaults against withering enemy fire, long route-marches across desert wastelands, thick serge uniforms, enormous packs that bowed soldiers down like old men – all these routines were to become the basis of the *règlement*. Small wonder, therefore, that more legionnaires died of heat exhaustion and of dysentery than from the tribesmen's bullets. Whole garrisons were decimated by sickness – 500 out of 750 at the fort of Miliana in Algeria; two complete battalions at Fondouk. At Fondouk, 207 men, including the colonel of the regiment, died at their posts, while 240 were carried away totally unfit for service.

The eventual conquest of North Africa was proof that the courage or endurance of disciplined soldiers can sometimes compensate for the

(*opposite above*) The 1836 attack on Constantine by 10,000 men, including a Legion battalion. (*below*) Death of General Damrémont during the second siege, 1837.

mistakes of their commanders. Luckily for the French, the converse
was also true: the brilliance of an enemy guerilla leader like Abd el-
Kader, the Berber chieftain, was often offset by the lack of disciplined
troops under his command. Abd el-Kader's tribesmen were certainly
brave; but they had no concept of organization, and fought as individual
and equal members of their particular Muslim brotherhood, coming
and going as they saw fit.

But the Berber leader's chances of victory were virtually eliminated
with the arrival of Thomas-Robert Bugeaud in 1841. Of Irish origin, a
private in Napoleon's army in 1804 and a Marshal of France forty years
later, Bugeaud was a professional soldier, with a professional's view:
namely, win your fight at all costs. Part of the cost was the annihilation
not only of the enemy soldier, but of his home, his family, and his means
of livelihood. Bugeaud, in short, introduced the concept of total war
into Algeria and found the Legion the ideal instrument for carrying out
his policy. The revolts were gradually crushed, forts were established
at strategic points, and roads were built ensuring good communications
throughout northern Algeria.

Today Algeria has one of the finest road systems in Africa, as it did,
for that matter, during the Roman occupation. The Third Augusta was
responsible for the Roman communications, the Foreign Legion for the
French network. The military roads gradually joined up the string of
forts which were eventually to reach from the Mediterreanean coast to
the Niger River, with outposts in many of the Saharan oases. These
early roads were tracks or *pistes* which the trans-Saharan traveller still
follows today in the remoter regions of the Great Desert.

And so, by 1870, the French were able to push their columns south
from Biskra (the 'Garden of Allah') and the other oases on the perimeter
of the desert into the Sahara proper. They hoped, in fact, to cross the
desert and to link up with their newly-acquired West African empire.
They were already thinking of a trans-Saharan railway, a dream that
was never to materialize.

One reason for the failure of the *trans-saharien* and for the slowness
of the conquest of the central Sahara was the obsession of the French
command with the old style of warfare in which massed columns of
infantry were trained to stand their ground in a square or to charge with
fixed bayonets across open terrain. It was obvious to anyone who knew
the desert and the tribes who lived there that such tactics were useless,
a lesson which even the most obtuse generals learnt when confronted
with the casualties in men and pack animals initially used in the attempted

(*left*) Thomas-Robert Bugeaud, the private in Napoleon's army who became a marshal of France. (*right*) Abd el-Kader, leader of the Berber tribesmen.

subjugation of the Sahara. The conventional armies, consisting of as many as four thousand camels, hundreds of horses and mules, and companies of men in thick woollen uniforms marching with packs weighing up to eighty pounds in temperatures of 115° Fahrenheit, soon became bogged down in the sand seas and were continually harassed by bands of Tuareg mounted on racing camels. These Tuareg, the Veiled Men of the Desert, proved formidable enemies and even when armed only with their *armes blanches*, the spear and shield made of hide, managed to delay the conquest, let alone the pacification, of the central Sahara for several decades.

Eventually it was the appearance on the scene in 1901 of an unusually intelligent officer that enabled the French to penetrate southwards into the Sahara at all. General François Henri Laperrine saw that mobility and not weight was the key to desert warfare. The Tuareg, on their swift racing camels, were mobile, even if they only had swords and leather shields to oppose the French rifles and cannon. Laperrine created the *Compagnies Méharistes*, or Camel Corps, to meet the Tuareg on their own terms, while General de Négrier formed the Foreign Legion's Mounted Companies, enabling the Legion to increase its day's march from twenty-five to forty miles by allotting one mule to two legionnaires who took it in turns to ride. These *Compagnies Montées* were to become the élite nucleus of the Legion in Africa before the

The Tuareg maintained control over the desert with sudden camel raids on the slow-moving French columns. They were defeated by General Laperrine's *méharistes* (Camel Corps) and the Mounted Companies of the Legion.

internal combustion engine put paid to mules, horses and, eventually camels.

It was the Mounted Companies of the Legion which enabled the French to hold their string of outposts along the frontiers of their newly-conquered territory, for the mule train could march, if necessary, fifty miles in a day, enabling relief forces to get through quickly to isolated forts under siege. These forts, which are still scattered throughout the old colonial empire, had scarcely changed in architectural style since the Third Augusta Legion built its outposts in the fourth century A.D. Indeed, the traveller in North Africa will have difficulty in differentiating between the ruins of a Roman fort like Bu N'gem in Libya and that of a French outpost like Fort Flatters in Algeria. Both are well built from the local stone, with solid walls crenellated and pierced with slots for firing; and both have corner watchtowers with ramparts for the sentries. Such fortresses were, of course, impregnable, provided a good look-out was kept, particularly at night, for the fortress walls were too high for the natives to climb and the guards too well protected by the parapet and the towers at each corner to be effectively shot at. The problem was always water, for if there was no well inside the fort, a water-party had to leave every other day for a supply point. Nearly all the battles which the Legion garrisons fought in the desert and mountains were holding-off attacks on the water-fatigue party or on the relief columns. Otherwise life was reasonably safe and secure inside the forts, and the principal danger was that boredom and the famous *cafard* would lead to a slackening in discipline. For this reason, the officer in command enforced the rules and regulations relentlessly – the duties of the sentinels, the sounding of reveille always at the precise moment, the sending out of an armed reconnaissance, the endless strengthening of the walls and towers, the organization of fatigue parties until, half an hour before nightfall, the 'Retreat' was sounded and every legionnaire came inside the fort.

Despite all the dangers and all the hardships of the Algerian war, the Legion had grown to identify itself with North Africa. Sidi-bel-Abbès was now their capital, their own city. The mountains and deserts were their homeland. They had made themselves into a formidable fighting unit and were beginning to be accepted as such even by the generals of the regular army. In fact the Legion was thought to be the answer to the French king Louis Philippe's problem of how to intervene in the Spanish Civil War.

The castle of Ksar Mara, deep in the Libyan desert, one of many ruined fortresses left behind by previous invaders of North Africa.

The Legion in Spain

The Legion disembarked at Tarragona on the North-east coast of Spain on 19 August 1835 to fight with the army of the infant Queen Isabella II (*above right*) against her rival to the throne, Don Carlos (*below right*). For the Legion, the Civil War consisted of a few major engagements, and frequent minor skirmishes, fought in the foothills of the Pyrenees, along a front stretching from Catalonia in the East to Navarre in the West. The Legion, becoming increasingly ill-equipped, ill-clothed, and ill-fed, was rushed from place to place as the Queen's troops advanced or retreated and eventually found themselves fighting a kind of guerilla warfare, sometimes without any real contact with the main forces. A major confrontation finally took place at the Battle of Barbastro (1838), where both sides fought with maniacal fury. Of the Carlist foreign legion only 160 men remained out of 875, and all the officers were killed or wounded. The French Foreign Legion was similarly decimated. When the war finally ended, more as a result of losses on both sides from disease than of positive victories on the field of battle, what was left of the Legion (222 officers and men), struggled across the Pyrenees into France on 8 January 1839.

The Spanish Campaign 1835-9

The obscure and long since forgotten Spanish Civil War of 1833–9 was fought between rival claimants for the throne – on the one hand, Isabella II, daughter of King Ferdinand VII, and on the other, Ferdinand's brother and Isabella's uncle, Don Carlos. Which of these two claimants should actually rule could have made little or no difference to the Spanish people, and it is difficult to see what difference it could have made to Britain and France, both of whom, however, intervened in the struggle. The British despatched to the Peninsula a so-called British Legion, consisting of some 10,000 men ordered to fight for Queen Isabella. It was stated by their commander, Sir George de Lacy Evans, that at least 2,200 of these conscripts were so crippled by disease or old age that they never reached the battlefield at all, which was just as well since neither the British nor the Spanish government had made any provision to feed and clothe them, or to furnish them with arms and ammunition.

The British decision to send troops in support of Isabella prompted Louis Philippe, the French king, to follow suit and so ensure that his country too was represented in the game of power politics. In 1835, however, Louis Philippe was short of manpower because of his war in North Africa, which was not proceeding very well. Moreover, like the British, he had no wish to waste good French soldiers on a Spanish domestic issue, particularly since the outcome was by no means certain. A legion of foreign troops was the obvious solution to his dilemma; and so in August 1835, much against their will, three battalions of Germans, Poles, Belgians, and Italians were transferred from Algeria to Spain.

When they disembarked at Tarragona in August 1835 they made a much better impression on the local population than they had done four years earlier when the citizens of Algiers laughed at their comic opera uniforms and unmilitary bearing. The Legion now marched well, though no doubt some eyebrows were raised to see not only their commander, Colonel Joseph-Nicolas Bernelle, at their head mounted on a horse, but his wife behind him, astride a mule, and behind her, Madame Bernelle's maid. However, the scene was not unusual in a period when a commanding officer's wife accompanied him to the wars.

The distinctive uniform of the Carlist
army: an officer and trooper (*right*).
Three engravings of the Spanish Civil
War from the loyalist point of view,
bearing the inscriptions: (*centre*) 'Thus
died Colonel Alonso, exhausted from
carrying on his shoulders weary soldiers
who were to be executed.' (*below*) 'The
survivors begged – as if it were a
privilege – to be shot with the others.'
(*far right*) 'Amidst the uproar and
carousing of Cabrera [Count of Morella,
Carlist leader] and his men the dreadful
volley was heard. The prisoners of Pla de
Pon were no more.'

Twenty years later, General Bazaine, the Commander of the Legion brigade sent to the Crimea, took both his beautiful Spanish wife and her piano with him. But to the rank and file disembarking at Tarragona, it was a matter of indifference who rode at the head of the parade, since they scarcely knew where they were going or for whom they were fighting.

However, the Legion, ordered to fight for Queen Isabella, proceeded to do so over the next four years with the efficiency which was to become its hallmark. Immediately after landing at Tarragona, the legionnaires were marched north to meet an unknown enemy in the mountains and valleys of Navarre. At first they were thrown into local skirmishes piecemeal, and found themselves fighting a guerilla war, not unlike that to which they had become accustomed in North Africa. On the other hand, they were not now fighting ill-armed and undisciplined tribesmen. Their own arms were, if anything, inferior to those of the Carlists, their principal weapon being an antiquated, muzzle-loading musket to which could be attached a bayonet. The muskets were inaccurate and the bayonets bent too easily, though they were adequate for their function of being thrust into an enemy's vitals. The legionnaires had also been issued with sabres, but these soon disappeared, sold by the hungry and unpaid troops or simply stolen. In addition, their uniforms were so garish that they could be seen for miles even on a dull day. The jackets were blue with either red, yellow, or green epaulettes, and the trousers were red. And as though to ensure that they could be seen from afar, the caps were high-crowned and bright red. This, at least, was how the legionnaires began the campaign. They finished it in rags.

But before the inglorious end, the Legion fought with characteristic

bravery, first in Catalonia along a line south of the Pyrenees, then to the
west, in Navarre around the city of Pamplona, and finally wherever the
Spanish army of Queen Isabella was in difficulties. The unit was used,
in other words, in what was to become its standard role in all subsequent
wars: as an assault force trained to die, if necessary to the last man.
There were many occasions during the battles and skirmishes of the
Spanish Civil War when the Legion seized victory from 'the jaws of
death' or avoided total defeat by defending a key position against enormous odds. But in the last analysis their courage and their sacrifices
made little difference to the outcome of a war which was not fought
according to any conventions or, for that matter, according to any known
principles of strategy, for neither side was capable of organizing its
troops behind the lines, let alone of directing them in battle. Such a war
could have gone on indefinitely if the casualties from dysentery, typhoid,
typhus, pneumonia, and starvation had not made the recruiting of new
troops almost impossible. Further, the atrocities on both sides eventually
reached a point where even the perpetrators agreed that they were
becoming intolerable.

The Foreign Legion, however, was lucky to survive it at all. Of the
9,000 men who had come to Spain, over 3,600 were either killed in
battle or died of their wounds. Some 150 officers were also killed or
wounded. Over 4,000 soldiers were 'missing', meaning that they
deserted, went over to the enemy (the Carlists also had a foreign legion
of their own), or crossed the Pyrenees into France. Nor is it at all surprising that nearly half the entire force deserted inasmuch as the men
were ill-fed, ill-clad, and ill-housed. Indeed, in the course of time as
they were shifted about from one battlefield to another, they began to
resemble more a troop of bandits than an army unit, at least in the eyes
of the local population whose homes and fields they pillaged.

In addition to the hardships the Legion had to endure in the field,
the officers were killed in such numbers that they could not be easily
replaced. Sometimes the commanders-in-chief did not, for one reason
or another, have the full confidence of their officers and men. The first
of them, Colonel Bernelle, although he was admired and even loved by
his men, was plagued with an interfering wife – she who insisted on
being at the head of the march past at Tarragona – a woman who was

The abandoned Fort Pacot in the Republic of Niger. Such forts enabled the
Legion to control the wells and caravan routes across the Sahara.

OPOL - 1854-55.

MEXIQUE - 1863. - CAPORAL DE GRENADIERS ET FUSILIER.

apparently detested by the legionnaires. A score of stories are recorded of this lady's interference in the day-to-day routine, typical of which was the fifteen days imprisonment she insisted should be inflicted on a soldier because he saw her in informal attire while he was working in her garden.

Colonel Bernelle was succeeded by a Major Jean-Louis Lebeau, a veteran of Napoleon's invasion of Russia and Waterloo. The major's appearance was the opposite of his name: evidently he looked more like Don Quixote than an army commander, for he wore an old tramp's hat, an ancient coat without the usual epaulettes, trousers which barely reached his knees, and a pair of broken boots to which were attached very long spurs. A huge Turkish scimitar hung from his shoulder by a length of string. Thus accoutred, Major Lebeau shuffled about with his eyes lowered as though afraid to look anyone in the face. The legionnaires were not impressed by their new commander, who was shortly replaced by a true Legion officer, Colonel Ludovic Conrad. Conrad fought and died according to the most chivalrous tradition of the Legion, galloping on a white charger ahead of his troops at the battle of Barbastro (1838), rallying them with his shouts of encouragement and his helmet held aloft on his cane. He was almost immediately shot dead. By this time, almost every officer of the Legion had been killed or wounded, and the men were demoralized. It was at this crucial moment that the French Foreign Legion came face to face with the foreign legion of Don Carlos. The two forces fought with maniacal fury, not calling off the engagement until they had practically wiped each other out. Of the Carlist foreign legion, 160 men remained out of 875. All their officers were dead or wounded. The French Foreign Legion had suffered comparable casualties. Contemporary historians state that the old Legion really ceased to exist at all after the battle at Barbastro; and their statements are not merely rhetorical, as can be seen from the statistics. On 19 August 1835, 5,000 legionnaires landed at Tarragona. During the next three and a half years, they were reinforced by another 4,000. On 8 January 1839 the following remnants of the Foreign Legion crossed the Spanish–French frontier:

63 officers

159 men

75 mules.

(above left) Captain Danjou exhorts his men to fight to the death at Camerone. *(above right and below)* Uniforms worn in Madagascar, the Crimea, and Mexico.

The Crimea 1854-6 · Italy 1859 Mexico 1863-7 · France 1870

The Crimea

One of the survivors of the Spanish campaign was François-Achille Bazaine, sergeant-major of the First Regiment of the Legion in 1832, brigadier-general during the Crimean campaign of 1855, Marshal of France in 1864, court-martialled and declared a traitor in 1870, imprisoned in 1873, condemned to death in 1874, escaped from jail in the same year, and died in straitened circumstances in Madrid in 1888 – an eventful career.

But what also distinguished Bazaine from his fellow generals in the Crimea was that he was only forty-three while most of them were nearer seventy; and, more important, he had seen a great deal of action in Africa and Spain while they had not been on a battlefield in decades. In fact, the decrepitude and inexperience of the supreme commanders in mid-nineteenth-century Europe were typical of the age, a classic example being Lord Raglan, commander-in-chief of the British forces in the Crimea, who had not heard a shot fired in anger since the Battle of Waterloo, forty-two years before.

Bazaine's legionnaires, too, were exceptional soldiers in view of their training and experience of actual combat. Yet as élite troops they were not really suitable for the war in which they were now engaged. For the Crimea, where Great Britain, France, and Turkey fought the Russians over spheres of influence in the Near East, was to foreshadow the most terrible war of all, that of 1914–18, a static trench war in which the sufferings and miseries of men forced to live like foxes in earths were only equalled by the unbelievable slaughter occasioned by 'set pieces': that is, the regular mass attacks which were as regularly anticipated by the enemy. The Legion, of course, was used as the spearhead of many of these assaults in the Crimea which were flung, regardless of losses, against almost impregnable positions. In fact, the military thinking of generals like Lord Raglan and Saint-Arnaud seemed to be based on the

General Canrobert (*inset*), commander of the French army in the Crimea, which fought before Sevastopol in the appalling conditions of trench warfare in winter.

theory that advances across hostile territory were best made in the manner that ants cross a river: namely, by moving irresistibly forward *en masse*, regardless of the cost in lives. The cost of the Battle of Inkermann (November 1854), for instance, was 35,000 killed; at Alma (September 1855), where the Legion was used to attack the Heights – a ridge on the south side of the river held by 40,000 Russians – the cost was not so high, only 10,000 killed or wounded. But the river was crossed and the Heights captured, and the Legion particularly distinguished itself by its heroism. 'Serve as examples to the others, brave legionnaires,' said General Canrobert.

After Alma, the Legion was used to spearhead the assaults on the Russian trenches outside Sevastopol and on the fortresses of the great military complex itself. The story was always the same. The generals ordered a strongpoint to be taken; the storm troops were led by the *étrangers* with fixed bayonets; and up the side of cliffs and over walls went the men in the classic frontal attack. Once within the enemy lines, the hand-to-hand fighting proceeded in much the same manner as in the wars of the Assyrians and Babylonians. Men literally hacked each other to pieces with their swords. No quarter was asked and none given. And in this kind of warfare, the Legion was unexcelled.

Before abandoning Sevastopol, the Russians burnt their fleet and attempted to burn the city itself. But there was still plenty left to loot when the allied armies burst in. The legionnaires showed themselves past masters at this. They had learnt the art in Algerian villages where, though there were not many items of value to carry off, most of the women wore heavy silver bracelets. It was not unknown for legionnaires to chop off a woman's hand in order to acquire her bracelets. In Sevastopol, in contrast, there were a number of much larger objects, like grandfather clocks, which the soldiers coveted and under which they were seen staggering along the streets, some wearing women's dresses and flowered hats over their uniforms, some carrying umbrellas and parasols, some dancing along with musical instruments under their arms. But the majority made straight for the wine cellars where they drank until they were insensible. The wine cellars of Sevastopol and the quantity of wine drunk in them became a legend of the Legion.

Italy

Once the Crimean war was over with a loss of nearly half a million men, the Legion was reorganized into two regiments, the First and Second, and sent back to North Africa. But by 1859, only three years after Crimea, Napoleon III decided to intervene in yet another conflict, whereupon the two regiments were recalled from Algeria and sent to Italy, to fight for Victor Emmanuel, King of Sardinia, against the Austrians. The French monarch had been promised the provinces of Nice and Savoy in return for military aid, though the political dealings behind the scenes were of no concern and of no interest to the legionnaires who landed at Genoa in April 1859. Those veterans who had survived Alma and Sevastopol probably hoped that Italy in the spring and summer would be a pleasant country in which to campaign. But while the terrain was certainly more hospitable than the frozen beaches of the Crimea or the torrid deserts of North Africa, the routine was the same as it had always been – long marches, inadequate rest, poor food and, finally, the commitment to battle.

It went without saying that the Legion was employed for the most dangerous assignments and consequently suffered its usual casualties, both of officers and men. At the Battle of Magenta (1859), a Lombardy market-town sixteen miles west of Milan, Colonel Chabrière, commanding the Second Regiment, led his men forward mounted on a white horse, holding his sword aloft, and shouting '*En avant*', thus offering himself as a target to the Austrian riflemen. He was killed by an Austrian bullet, and immediately replaced by his second in command Major Martinez, who led his legionnaires into the centre of Magenta where they fought it out with the Austrian defenders from house to house and room to room, the officers using their swords, the men their bayonets.

A few weeks after Magenta, at Solferino, the Legion was again committed as the advance assault force, and the Second Regiment, now commanded by Colonel Martinez, was given the task of clearing a cemetery of Austrian sharpshooters. Legion battle flags celebrate a victory both at Solferino and at Magenta, although its exploits are not even mentioned in the standard history of the Italian campaign.[1] Perhaps this is understandable when one considers the enormity of the Battle of Solferino which saw the employment of 300,000 men, 50,000 horses, and 2,600 cannon on a front thirteen miles long.

When the Italian war ended in the late summer of 1859, the Legion was sent to Paris to take part in the victory parade. For this occasion they were issued with new uniforms and presented with thirty-five decorations for bravery. They were aroused at two o'clock in the morning in order to be ready for the march past at ten o'clock. As soon as the parade was over, they were ordered to leave Paris without a moment's

The Emperor Napoleon III (*inset*) witnessed the battle of Solferino during the Italian war of 1859, and was appalled by the enormous loss of life.

delay, to be shipped off again to North Africa. 'Foreign Legion' was still a distasteful expression both to the French government and the civilian population. In fact, attempts were now made to disband the Legion altogether, for a ministerial decree of 1861 ordered the suspension of further enlistment of foreigners and recommended the repatriation of legionnaires with only two or more years to serve. This sudden and uncharacteristic manifestation of an anti-military spirit on the part of Napoleon III was said to be due to the 'glorious victory' at Solferino, with its 40,000 casualties of which 12,000 were French, including five generals, seven colonels, six lieutenant-colonels, and some 700 other officers killed outright. Napoleon, who had personally witnessed the carnage, had been shocked. But he soon recovered his nerve. Other opportunities for war and glory presented themselves, this time across the Atlantic in Mexico.

Mexico

French interests in Mexico were primarily political, for all the European monarchs agreed that 1) republican Mexico was in a state of chaos and needed 'regeneration'; and 2) it was essential to prevent the United States from undertaking that 'regeneration'. The British having declined to become overtly involved, Napoleon III agreed to undertake the task himself in 1861. His pretext for intervention was the refusal of the Mexican government to pay its debts. His plan was to place the Austrian Archduke Ferdinand Maximilian on a throne specially created for him by a coalition of European monarchs: namely, Napoleon of France, Franz Joseph of Austria, Leopold of Belgium, and Victoria of England. In addition, Napoleon provided the army required to crush the republicans; and the spearhead of this force was to be the Foreign Legion.

At first Napoleon's venture seemed to be succeeding as his troops occupied most of the principal cities in the south, including Vera Cruz, the chief port, and Mexico City, the capital. The forces of Benito Juarez, the pure-bred Indian leader of the Mexican nationalist movement, continued, however, to operate in the mountains and swamps beyond the reach of the French regulars. As was so often the case in the colonial wars of the nineteenth century, it was the terrain and the endemic diseases which were the chief enemies of the invaders. The Legion, which had been assigned the most fever-stricken regions to patrol, began to be debilitated by malaria and dysentery; and losses from these diseases partly explains what happened in the year 1863 at a village called Camerone on the road between Vera Cruz and Mexico City.

Camerone! It is the most evocative name in Legion history, even though it will not be found on any but the largest-scale maps. Yet it is important to know what happened on 30 April 1863 at the farmhouse whose ruins, visible until a few years ago, inspired this inscription on a marble plaque placed among the other trophies of war in Les Invalides in Paris:

QUOS HIC NON PLUS LX
ADVERSI TOTIUS AGMINIS
MOLES CONSTRAVIT
VITA PRIUS QUAM VIRTUS
MILITES DESERVIT GALLICOS
DIE XXX MENSI APR. ANNI MDCCCLXIII

(Those who lie here, though less than sixty in number, fought an entire army before being overwhelmed by sheer weight. Life abandoned these French soldiers before honour did on the 30th of April, 1863.)

These few words epitomize the story of Captain Jean Danjou, thirty-five years old, veteran of the Crimea, Italy, and North Africa, and his

QUOS HIC NON PLUS LX
ADVERSI TOTIUS AGMINIS
MOLES CONSTRAVIT

The hamlet of Camerone, the scene of
the most celebrated of the Legion's
exploits, lies on the old highway
between the port of Vera Cruz on the
Gulf of Mexico and Mexico City, the
Aztec as well as the modern capital of
the country. In 1863 the railway link
between the two cities had not been
completed, so all military and other
supplies had to go by road. The convoys
were under constant attack from the
Nationalist troops as the wagons wound
their way through the foothills of the
Sierra Madre, and the whole length of
the trail had to be protected by French
army units. The Legion was responsible
for the section between Vera Cruz and
Puebla; and it was about halfway along this
stretch, at a farmhouse in the village of
Camerone, that Captain Danjou with his
company of legionnaires held off some
2,000 Mexican attackers (*far right*). The
Captain and most of his men died in the
farmhouse, but the convoy, bringing
arms, ammunition, and gold, got through
safely to Mexico City. The gallantry of
Captain Danjou and his men has made
'Camerone' the most evocative name in
the annals of the Legion. Every year on
30 April, Danjou's wooden hand –
recovered from the ruins of the Mexican
farmhouse and today the most treasured
relic of the corps – is honoured by a
solemn military parade.

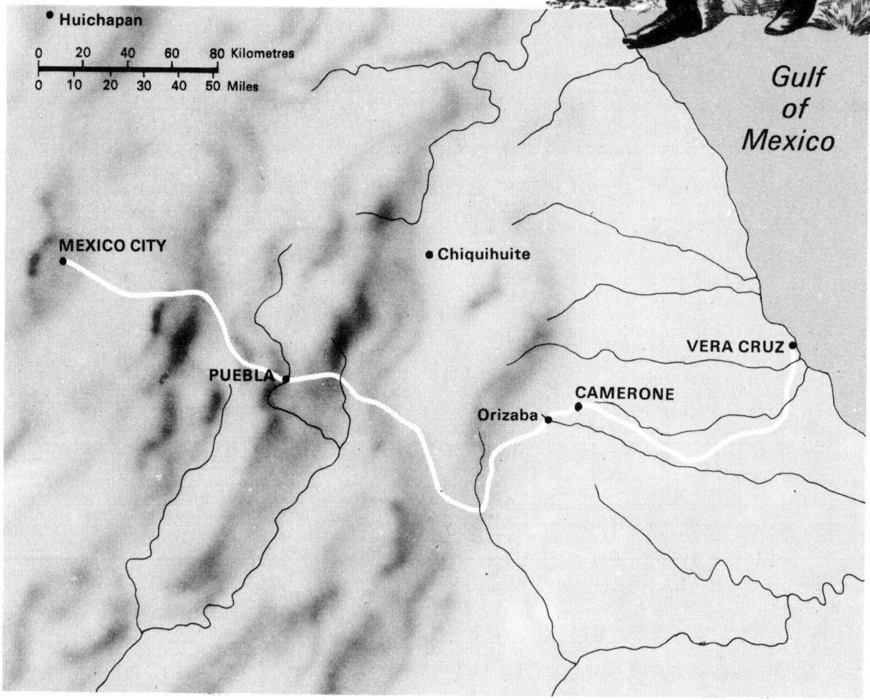

Huichapan

0   20   40   60   80 Kilometres
0   10   20   30   40   50 Miles

*Gulf
of
Mexico*

MEXICO CITY

Chiquihuite

VERA CRUZ

PUEBLA

CAMERONE

Orizaba

company of sixty-four men – men with names like Bartolotto, Katau, Wenzel, Kunassek, Gorski. Captain Danjou's orders were to keep open the highway connecting Vera Cruz and Mexico City so that the French could send through a convoy of 60 carts and 150 mules carrying arms, ammunition, and three million francs in gold to headquarters in the capital.

For this purpose he volunteered to lead a depleted company of sixty-two men together with two officers from another unit on a reconnaissance mission along the Vera Cruz–Puebla road. He had volunteered for this assignment because the commanding officer and fifty men of the Third Company were all ill with malaria or dysentery. So with his under-strength company, Danjou left camp at one o'clock in the morning and, marching all night, reached high ground at seven in the morning when it was decided to brew up coffee. The Legion troop had, in the meantime, been observed by the Mexicans whose leader, Colonel Milan, now decided to wipe them out before attacking the convoy coming from Vera Cruz.

As soon as he was harassed by the Mexican cavalry, Captain Danjou withdrew his men to a farmhouse in the village of Camerone, no doubt hoping to be able to hold off sporadic attacks by small groups of horse-men until the main body of the Legion came to his relief. But he was mistaken; within a matter of hours, his company was besieged by a small army of at least 2,000 men – 300 regular cavalry, 350 guerillas, and three battalions of infantry. Of his own company of sixty-four, sixteen were already dead, wounded, or missing, leaving only three officers and forty-six legionnaires to defend the farmhouse. They could not hope to survive against such odds, which may explain why Captain Danjou, before he died, demanded that each of them take an oath to fight to the end. The end came in the evening after a day of non-stop fighting during which the defenders had had nothing to eat and, worse, nothing to drink. By six o'clock the original company of three officers and sixty-two men was reduced to one officer, Second-lieutenant Maudet, and eleven legionnaires. The others were either dead or badly wounded, among them Captain Danjou, shot in the head, and his second-in-command, Lieutenant Vilain, mortally wounded. Soon after six the Mexicans decided on an all-out attack on the barn urged on by Colonel Milan who realized that to lose this battle would be a lasting disgrace to the Mexican army and the cause of liberation. This time the assault was overwhelming. But as the Mexicans swarmed in through the now un-defended windows and doors of the farmhouse, Lieutenant Maudet ordered a bayonet charge. At the head of his four remaining legion-naires, he rushed out into the courtyard to meet the cross-fire of the besiegers and fell, hit in the face and body. One of his men was shot dead in this last charge; the other three were taken prisoner. The battle in the farmhouse at Camerone had lasted nine hours, and when it was over, two officers and twenty legionnaires were dead; one officer and twenty-two legionnaires were wounded; and twenty legionnaires had been taken prisoner. The Mexican casualties were around three hundred. The Third Company of the Second Battalion of the Legion had been wiped out, but the convoy of arms and money passed through without incident and reached Mexico City safely.

Camerone was symbolic – 'a glorious defeat' on the one hand, a 'glorious victory' on the other. The defeat was the loss of a company of sixty-five professional fighting-men; the victory was the saving of the convoy. But there were very few opportunities in Mexico for the *bravura* of Camerone: on the contrary, the casualties among the Legion were mostly the result of disease and the inevitable desertions. The final toll was thirty-one officers and 1,917 men dead or missing out of 4,000 sent to Mexico during the four years of Maximilian's reign.

Once the French troops had been withdrawn by order of Napoleon, who was becoming increasingly apprehensive of United States inter-vention on the side of the Mexican insurgents, the imperial régime quickly collapsed. Maximilian the emperor lost the last battle at Queretaro and was shot by a Mexican firing-squad on 19 June 1867. He was thirty-five years old. His wife, Marie Charlotte Amélie Augustine-Victoire Clémentine Léopoldine, the empress Carlota, went mad in 1866 and died in 1927, aged eighty-seven. Her madness was said to have been induced by the decision of Napoleon to abandon her husband to his fate.

France

But the French emperor was no longer in a position to help the man he had made emperor. The Americans were threatening him in Mexico, the Germans on the Rhine. On 19 July 1870 he declared war on Germany. Exactly two months later, the Germans were at the gates of Paris. In the capital itself, the Third Republic was proclaimed and every available man was summoned from the provinces at home and overseas to make up one more army, the Army of the Loire. Two battalions of the Foreign Legion were recalled from Africa, to fight on French soil for the first time. At Besançon they held off the Germans long enough for 80,000 defeated French regulars to cross the frontier into Switzerland.

By January 1871 the French had been ignominiously defeated, the emperor Napoleon III had been deposed, and a civil war between the royalists and the republicans had begun. This war was fought most fiercely in the streets of Paris even while the German army was besieging the capital.

The last act of the Legion in France was to crush the revolt of the Parisians. The Legion was called in by the Thiers government to lead the Army of Versailles into Paris, since it was feared by this time that no prisoners would be taken by either side and no quarter given. This was how the Legion was accustomed to fight. General Edmé Patrice MacMahon, the hero of Magenta and himself an ex-Legion officer, ordered the attack. The Legion obeyed. No prisoners were taken; and the *communards* of Paris saw to it that their dead were revenged. They began to shoot priests, nuns, politicians, and any government soldiers they could capture. In the meantime, the Legion stormed their barricades and fought its way to the heart of Paris. By the end of May 1871 the Paris revolution had been crushed, some 30,000 Parisians had been killed, the Legion had suffered heavy casualties, and the corps, now hated and feared by the civilian population, was hastily withdrawn and shipped back to Algeria.

The Sahara·Dahomey·Madagascar 1871-96

The Sahara

What was left of the Legion after the war of 1870–1 came back to Algeria in June of the latter year, to remain in and to be identified with North Africa for almost the next hundred years. Indeed, to the outside world, North Africa, and particularly the Sahara, is the country of the French Foreign Legion. And to the traveller in this immense and awesome desert, the lost and abandoned ruins of the Legion's forts still standing in the sand seas are the monuments of a past glory.

The years between 1871 and 1939 saw the whole of France's four million square miles of African territory conquered, explored, secured, and developed, so that there was no corner of the Sahara itself that was not safe from the religious fanatics, warring tribesmen, and camel-riding bandits of the preceding period. Even the formidable Tuareg, or Veiled Men of the Desert, had been subdued and regarded the French, if not as friends, at least as worthy of respect. The old hatreds, fed by fanatical marabouts, seem to have faded away as the bulk of the tribes accepted the inevitability of French colonial rule which, they admitted, had brought a number of benefits to their country. The desire and demand for freedom and independence were to come later, with the spreading of liberal ideas throughout the colonial world between the two world wars.

The role of the Legion in this slow and relentless conquest of the Sahara was first to clean out nests of resistance, and then to man the strongpoints by which the French hoped to control and eventually pacify the desert. The actual battles of this period were principally a series of continual minor engagements between bands of hostile tribesmen on the one side and detachments of the Legion on the other.

Captain Robert Lefort, *alias* Robert-Philippe-Louis-Eugène-Ferdinand, d'Orléans, duc de Chartres, describes a typical Legion expedition in 1871. The column, known by the men who went on it as *La Colonne*

Captain Robert Lefort, prince d'Orléans and duc de Chartres, visits a field hospital in the Sahara.

de la soif, left the oasis of Ouargla, recently captured by the French, and pushed on south into the open desert in pursuit of a band of rebellious tribesmen. The report tells how the column set off with provisions for nineteen days, with guides who were not properly familiar with the country, and without maps. The detachments marched or rode twenty-two miles under a full sun the first day in order to reach the well at Bou Rouba, only to find that the fleeing tribesmen had filled it with sand. The horses could not be watered. Moreover, as they were preparing to camp for the night, a courier arrived with the news that the vanguard of the column had made contact with the enemy and needed support. The French commander's native troops had started to desert him. The Legion now marched on most of the night and reached the next well, El Guara, at two o'clock in the morning. This well was almost dry. There was not enough water to make coffee. In addition, the guide admitted he did not know where they were. At daybreak, they marched south again and at eleven o'clock reached the wells at Mezuerda. It took four hours to water the horses and fill the water-skins. And so the column pursued the enemy as far south as the oases called Tamesguida and Aïn Teiba. The tribesmen, mounted on camels, simply melted into the distance. But the revolt had been quelled and the French penetration pushed farther south.

New forts and new roads were built by the Legion, and it was from this period, the end of the nineteenth century, that the entire Sahara could be said not only to have been conquered but also to have been pacified by the French. A region once as remote and mysterious to the western world as the surface of the moon was now thrown open to the ordinary tourist as well as the explorer and scientist, and it was possible by the early decades of the new century to cross safely and in a few weeks a desert which fifty years before had taken the lives of thousands of soldiers and almost every civilian who attempted to penetrate it.[1] There were now two main north–south highways across the desert, the easterly and more difficult one known as the Hoggar route; the westerly, the Tanezrouft route. Both were lines of communication between Algeria and West Africa where the French had acquired another vast colonial empire, which now included Mauritania, Senegal, Guinea, the Ivory Coast, Dahomey, the Sudan, and Niger (*see map page 30*).

In many of the campaigns which had to be fought in the far corners of the new empire, the Legion was in the vanguard, particularly in Indo-China, Dahomey, and Madagascar. Indeed, these campaigns and those days constituted the golden age of the Foreign Legion, which acquired such renown as the élite corps of the French army that service in it became the first choice of the top cadets of the military academies. It never again lacked for the best officers and volunteers.

Dahomey

The civilian world, both in France and elsewhere, was particularly interested in such African campaigns as that fought by the Legion in Dahomey in 1892, since this 'Expedition' (as the French euphemistically called the war) proved to be as exotic as any in military history, due to the participation of black Amazons who fought in regular military formations. And whereas the Amazons of classical times, though frequently depicted in Greek art and literature, must be dismissed as mythological, there was no denying the existence of the women warriors of Dahomey.

All this became apparent when, in 1892, the French sent an expeditionary force of European and colonial troops to Dahomey.

In those days, Dahomey was a relatively unknown African kingdom, although already partially opened up by British, German, and French traders. Most of it was forest, the whole region scarcely mapped at all. The conquest of such territory called for careful planning based not on any particular military strategy but on moving a small striking force along bush paths through forests and swamps to the capital of the country at Abomey. Here the king had his palace, his treasury, his household, and his army, the hard core of which were the regiments of women who naturally added to the interest of the forthcoming campaign. Were there such creatures as genuine Amazons? What did they look like? How did they conduct themselves in battle?

There had been a great deal of speculation about these women warriors until Sir Richard Burton visited West Africa in 1861 and gave an eye-witness account of the Dahomean Amazons:

[They are] mostly remarkable for a stupendous stratopyga and for a development of adipose tissue which suggested anything but ancient virginity. . . . I saw old, ugly, and square-built frows [*fraus*], trudging 'grumpily' along, with the face of 'cook' after being much 'knagg'd' by 'the missus'.[2]

Of these 'frows' he estimates there were some 1,700 divided into groups whom he classifies as:

1. The blunder-buss women who may be considered the grenadiers. They

are the biggest and strongest of the force, and each is accompanied by
an attendant carrying ammunition. With the blunder-buss women rank
the carbineers, the Sure-to-kill Company, and the bayoneteers.

2. The elephant huntresses, who are held to be the bravest.
3. The razor women, who seem to be simply an *épouvantail* [scarecrows].
4. The infantry, forming the staple force from which the élite is drawn.
   They are armed with muskets and are well supplied with bad ammunition. They 'manoeuvre with the precision of a flock of sheep', and they
   are too light to stand a charge of the poorest troops in Europe. Personally, they are cleanly made, without much muscle; they are hard
   dancers, indefatigable singers, and though affecting a military swagger,
   their faces are anything but ferocious – they are rather mild and un-
   assuming in appearance.
5. The archeresses – the parade corps . . . They are distinguished by scanty
   attire, by a tatoo extending to the knee, and by an ivory bracelet on the
   left arm . . . When in the field they are used as scouts and porters.[3]

It is clear from Burton's description of the Amazon army that he did not
hold a very high opinion of their military prowess. Consistent with his
cool, impersonal analysis of primitive peoples, he notes that the Dahomean soldier, whether male or female, is not distinguished for training,
discipline, or equipment; and in any case, the object of his warfare was
to capture slaves, not to kill enemies. But, he says, 'the women are as
brave as, if not braver than, their brethren in arms, who certainly do not
shine in that department of manliness'.[4]

In consequence, the Dahomean kings who were traditionally the
commanders-in-chief of their armies, invariably used their women
soldiers as assault troops. It was the Legion, the spearhead of the
invasion forces, who had to stand the brunt of the Amazons' attacks,
which were mounted with a sort of desperation or, according to some
observers, under the influence of gin, the evidence of which was supposed to be the number of empty gin bottles found on and around the
battlefields. But whatever the reason for their recklessness, the Amazons
proved formidable adversaries in the series of minor pitched battles
which the invaders had to fight on their march to the capital. It was the
kind of warfare in which a soldier was liable to have his nose *bitten* off in
close quarter fighting.

However, the suicidal attacks by the Dahomeans, the Amazons in the
vanguard, against the French formations were repulsed with a great loss

(*above*) Abomey, the capital city, with its palace and treasury, was burnt to the
ground before the Legion captured it in August 1893. (*below*) A state reception
given by the king to a white trader.

of life to the attackers and the minimum casualties to the defenders. At the Battle of Poguessa, for instance, the Dahomeans lost 200 dead, of whom twenty were Amazons, to the loss of eight European and native soldiers. The Africans were to suffer even greater losses when the Legion was ordered to charge with fixed bayonets. A legionnaire describes these charges, the very essence of the Legion's battle tactics, as depressing and even demoralizing, when they were made against the Amazons. Yet even though their own battlefield losses were slight, continual thirst, sleepless nights, the clouds of mosquitoes, and armies of red ants left the men in no mood to feel sentimental about women-soldiers. They advanced steadily through the dense forests, fighting off continual

(*below*) Beheadings were a regular feature of public life in Dahomey. (*right*) An Amazon: Sir Richard Burton, who visited Dahomey in 1861, admired neither the looks nor the martial prowess of these women warriors.

attacks and burning captured villages. By August 1893, the vanguard of the Legion's troops had reached the capital, Abomey, only to find the king's palace and the entire settlement burnt to the ground. King Behanzin himself had burnt his capital before fleeing to the north where, from various hideaways, he continued for a time to issue proclamations avowing that he and his people would die to the last man rather than surrender.

Such rhetoric was ignored, and the Legion was given the job of tracking down the fugitive king. With a company of Senegalese, they chased him from village to village, while his brother was elevated to the throne by the French. This was the end for Behanzin who, deserted by his last supporters, surrendered on 25 January 1894. He was incarcerated on the French island of Martinique, together with four of his wives, their four children, a Dahomean prince, the prince's wife, and an interpreter.

The conquest of Dahomey had cost the French little in either Frenchmen's lives or money. The expeditionary army was never greater than some 4,000 men, of whom 795 were Europeans, the rest native troops. But some idea of who did the brunt of the fighting and who, therefore, was responsible for the victory is seen in the statistics of the killed and wounded among the European troops.[5]

	Killed	Wounded	Total
Foreign Legion	131	118	249
All other units	89	217	306

Legion casualties included their commander, Major Marius Faurox, and almost one out of two officers and men, though the fearsome diseases of West Africa – yellow fever, typhoid, malaria, enteric dysentery, and so forth – accounted for more losses than the fighting itself. In the end, of the 800 legionnaires sent to Dahomey, only 450 returned to the base camp at Sidi-bel-Abbès.

Madagascar

In the same year as the conquest of Dahomey, the French invaded the island of Madagascar on the opposite side of the continent. Madagascar had been a sort of French protectorate since the mid-seventeenth century when the *Compagnie de l'Orient*, the French equivalent of the East India Company, set up trading posts on the island. The British, busy during the same and later periods in getting possession of Zanzibar to the north, were not overtly opposed to the French occupation of Madagascar, particularly as their rivals were having continual difficulties in subduing the natives, because, according to French sources, the British used their missionaries 'to stir up an odious campaign against us right up to 1895'.[6]

Towards the end of 1894, the French declared war on Madagascar which was then a country of a half-a-dozen primitive tribes, partly African, partly Indonesian, of whom the Hovas were the dominant group. The Hovas were said to have an army of 40,000 men equipped with rifles, field pieces, and several batteries of cannon – theoretically a formidable force were it not for the fact that in order to conserve ammunition, the soldiers were forbidden to fire their weapons. Indeed, when it eventually came to discharging their guns, the artillerymen simply fired them at point blank range, since they did not know how to use the sighting mechanism.

The Malagasy army, in short, resembled a comic opera force by

(*inset*) A Hova general in full dress, one of the commanders of the Malagasy army of 40,000 men. Although trained by British officers, the emphasis seems to have been more on resplendent uniforms than on strategy and tactics, so there was little real resistance when the French invaded Madagascar with 14,000 men in 1894. (*below*) An encampment of the Malagasy army.

ECPA

Colonel Shervinton (*far right*), one of two British commanders of the Malagasy army, with his native officers. He left Madagascar before the French invasion.

European standards, the emphasis being upon the splendour of the officers' uniforms rather than on training or discipline: a lieutenant, for example, had five gold stripes on his sleeve, a general eleven, and a field-marshal seventeen. Their commanders-in-chief were two English soldiers-of-fortune, General Digby Willoughby and Colonel Charles Robert St Leger Shervinton, both of whom had fought in South Africa in the Zulu and Basuto wars. A correspondent of the *Manchester Guardian* who witnessed Willoughby and Shervinton training levées at a military camp sent home this report:

> We saw several of the companies put through their various drills, and were much struck with the smartness, physique, &c of some of the regiments.
>
> Colonel Shervinton said that, could he have a certain one of these regiments for a year, he would not be afraid of any crack regiment in the world.
>
> The men continued drill until 5. After that, the General and Colonel Shervinton went pigeon-shooting, and brought down nineteen out of twenty birds.[7]

This pair of typical Victorian adventurers disappeared from the Malagasy scene before the French invasion. General Willoughby was arrested in London for debt and on his return to Madagascar court-martialled for malfeasance; Colonel Shervinton left his post and returned to England where he died in obscurity, aged forty-five.

Obviously their presence would not have made the slightest difference to the outcome of the war once the French decided to send a force of some 14,000 men, including a battalion of the Legion. This army was supported at sea by a flotilla of eleven warships led by the cruiser *Primauguet* and on land by sixty-four horses, 6,620 mules, and over a thousand carts. The planners in Paris evidently had no idea of the country in which they were proposing to campaign, since carts were useless in a land without a single road.

The huge top-heavy French invasion army was an object of ridicule to foreign observers and of alarm to the French army doctors, since the obvious lesson of the Dahomey campaign which had just ended was that white soldiers could not withstand the tropical climate and diseases of Africa. It was, therefore, self-evident that to take an army of young men fresh from the towns and villages of a temperate land and to put them down in the jungles of an island in the Indian Ocean was a stupid and expensive way in which to subjugate a primitive people. Even the commanding general, Jacques-Charles-René-Achille Duchesne, formerly a lieutenant-colonel in the Foreign Legion, must have been aware of this, for in his invocation to the troops he stressed that the actual fighting must be quickly over. What the soldiers would really be up against was disease, and 'for me,' he added, 'the best-commanded corps will be that which has the fewest sick.' Evidently his exhortation fell on deaf ears. Within a month of their arrival sixty per cent of the expeditionary force were unfit for active duty. One year later 5,000 soldiers were dead, not casualties of war, but of disease. The official report of the surgeon-general declares:

> Despite their indomitable energy, despite their sacrifices without relief during the last three months, the young soldiers are beginning to show signs of demoralization: a large number of suicides are taking place in the hospitals and in the field. . . .
> It is not unusual to see men dragging themselves along at the rear of a column nearly dead with dysentery or fever, with enormously swollen and ulcerated legs. When the sun rose over the camp, they were found lying stiffly on the ground: they were dead.[8]

As for the Legion, such was its reputation that General Gallieni, the first governor-general, is reported to have requested the War Minister to let him have at least one battalion of the Legion with him in Madagascar 'so that, if the occasion arises, I can die honourably'.

The French in Indo-China

The French began their penetration of Indo-China in the mid-nineteenth century with various commercial treaties and para-military expeditions, starting in the South in Cochin China and gradually extending their control northwards. By 1883 they had more or less conquered the five nations which were to become known as French Indo-China; and the Legion was now brought over from Africa in force to patrol and pacify the vast territory, to establish strongpoints, build roads, and deal with sporadic outbreaks of rebellion. The Legion stayed on in Indo-China right up to the Second World War, when the colony was overrun by the Japanese. Re-formed after the war, the Legion began again the task of pacifying the colony which was now openly hostile to the French occupation. After eight years of almost continuous warfare, the end came with the fall of the great military bastion at Dien Bien Phu in 1954.

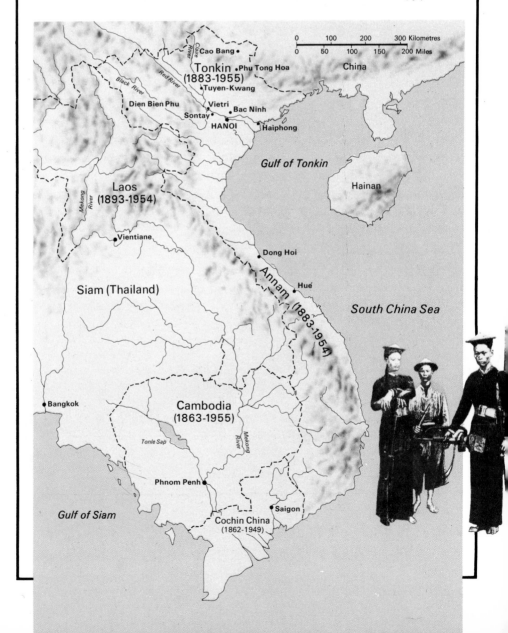

Indo-China 1883-91

Despite their rivalries and deep hostilities, the European powers were prepared tacitly to recognize spheres of influence and areas of conquest. Thus Madagascar had been left to the French, Zanzibar to the British. The latter, firmly entrenched in India and Burma, were disposed to allow the former a fairly free hand in Indo-China. As for China itself, it was considered large enough to be classified as open territory, and all the great powers picked off what they wanted along the commercially profitable coast.

The French penetration of Indo-China had begun in the eighteenth century when the first explorers, merchants, and missionaries established themselves in Cochin China, the southern region of South Vietnam. There had been trouble with the missionaries, and as early as 1858, a French expedition had been sent to Cochin China to punish the inhabitants for their opposition to the Church. The punishment consisted of seizing most of the province of Annam and putting it under French protection.

Annam, like the contingent provinces of Tonkin to the north and Laos and Cambodia to the west, was really a Chinese protectorate, theoretically ruled by petty kings, viceroys, and mandarins, but actually controlled by bands of mercenaries captained by rival warlords. Consequently the political and civil situation throughout the whole region was chaotic, and to civilized foreigners the warlords were so many bandits whose suppression was in the best interests of all concerned. There was, then, no difficulty in justifying the necessity to send in an expeditionary force to make the area safe for religion and commerce.

Any such operation in particularly difficult territory now automatically involved the Legion; and so on 27 September 1883 the First Battalion of the First Regiment left Sidi-bel-Abbès for the Far East. The Legion was to be involved in the conquest and pacification of Indo-China for almost the next hundred years. In fact, Indo-China was to be the location of some of their greatest triumphs and greatest defeats.

But in the beginning, in the winter of 1883, the French anticipated no great problems in defeating opponents who were, in the end, ill-led and ill-equipped, a motley collection of medieval warriors led by local barons

French troops in Indo-China (Tonkin): (*left to right*) sailor fusilier, marine artillery, marine infantry, foreign legionnaire, Algerian rifles.

interested only in pillage and looting. Wandering about the undefended countryside, massed behind huge red, yellow and black banners, sometimes allied with the Chinese soldiery, sometimes opposing them, they terrorized rich and poor alike, exacting treasure and taxes, accountable to nobody but themselves. There were tens of thousands of these *Pavillons Noirs*, or Black Flags, for it was an easy life for an able-bodied man who had the choice of joining the land armies or the river pirates. It was easy, that is, until he met disciplined troops, like Admiral Courbet's 5,000 soldiers, supported by a naval flotilla. The admiral had no difficulty in reducing such forts as the Black Flags' stronghold at Sontay, north-west of Hanoi. Of these irregulars, 25,000 had blockaded themselves in this citadel, which was a splendid example of Chinese military architecture with moat, bamboo fence, parapet, brick walls, and massive gates enclosing a small city of pagodas, barracks, shops, and the rest. Over the fortress floated the great silk flags of the barons and from within came the continuous beating of bells and gongs. The French soldiery was not, of course, interested in this extraordinary spectacle, and the Legion, which was naturally given the job of making a frontal assault, had no time to ponder the curiosities of oriental military architecture, but stormed the citadel in the following fashion:

> Despite the hail of bullets, our brave soldiers advanced just the same; many of them were hit and fell; but nothing could diminish their ardour. Captain Mehl of the Foreign Legion fell mortally wounded just as his men, newly arrived at the foot of the rampart, got a footing on the parapet. A soldier called Minnaert [*sic*] of the Legion was the first to enter the fort.[1]

And so the Legion was once again in the van of the attack. A Legion officer was among the first to be killed, no doubt because he over-exposed himself in urging on his men, and a Legion soldier made the grand gesture of planting the *tricolore* on the fortress walls. At the same time, a small force of French assault troops was able to break into a stoutly built fortress defended by an estimated 25,000 men with the loss of only a handful of soldiers killed and wounded. The explanation of such a facile victory is simple: the French had artillery and professional soldiers, the Black Flags had an assortment of weapons, most of which were obsolete, and a huge mob of undisciplined cut-throats. In February 1884 the French attacked the second Black Flag stronghold

Chinese engraving (1883) depicting an imaginary recapture of the Black Flag stronghold at Sontay, actually taken and held by Legion assault troops.

General de Négrier, a veteran of the Legion and commander in Indo-China, employed large forces of French troops and coolies to reduce the Black Flag forts.

at Bac Ninh, this time with 5,000 troops and 6,000 coolies under the command of General de Négrier. The fort was defended by 15,000 Tonkinese stiffened with Chinese regulars. Once again the Legion breached the fortifications and once again the redoubtable Mammaert planted the flag on the ramparts. (The Englishman George Manington served with this Belgian corporal whom he calls Mertens and describes as being 6ft 4in. and 'broad in proportion'.[2])

It would, however, be unrealistic to underestimate the difficulties of conquering a region as complex as Indo-China. The area consists of some 300,000 square miles of mountain, jungle, swamp, and deltas, which a hundred years ago was without any roads at all. Communications depended upon the rivers, transport upon native bearers or coolies. Resistance to the French conquest, then, came not from the people, apart from the warlords and their Chinese allies, but from the terrain and, above all, the endemic diseases: malaria, amoebic dysentery, cholera, typhus, and typhoid. Besides these, venereal diseases, alcoholism, and opium took an equally high toll of the invaders' health. Even though the fighting from the Legion's point of view was no more arduous than it had been in Africa, and certainly less hazardous than on the European battlefields, service in Indo-China was not an assignment either soldiers or civilians looked forward to. Mindful of the legionnaires' fears of catching some exotic disease and of their hesitancy about volunteering for service in the East, the High Command offered extra pay, extra food, and extra wine, and an additional ration of rum as incentives. Besides these concessions, the legionnaires soon discovered another compensation for the hazards and rigours of the country. Women were theirs for the taking; not the wretched whores of the Algerian brothels, but graceful girls prepared to be loving and faithful consorts – the *congais*, as they were called. Reared in the eastern tradition of total subservience to their men, these petite Vietnamese made a home for the soldiers behind the lines and even followed them to the battlefront. The authorities had no objection to a legionnaire keeping a home when he went off duty, though they began to be concerned when the soldiers, with the encouragement of their wives, fell into the opium habit. For the ceremony of the evening smoke was as much a part of life in the East as afternoon tea was in nineteenth-century England, and it is described by George Manington in considerable detail.

Tho [the Tonkinese sergeant attached as an interpreter to the Legion battalion at Nha Nam] would lie on his right side, a hollow block of green-

Opium smoking, was widespread throughout the East. Soldiers were sometimes introduced to the habit by their *congai*, or Vietnamese mistress.

enamelled earthenware serving as a pillow beneath his head. His wife would stretch out opposite to and facing him. Between them was placed the tray with its little implements, and the lamp was lit. This was the solemn moment of the day.[3]

The Legion now had two battalions on active duty in Indo-China, and they were used in every campaign for the eight years (1883–91) during which the French fought to gain control of the area until five separate nations were considered pacified. The five nations were Cochin China, Annam, Tonkin, Laos, and Cambodia, eventually united in a federation within the French colonial empire.

The last serious attempt by the Black Flags, with the aid of the Chinese, to overcome the invaders led to the siege of a jungle fort which was ominously prophetic of what was to take place sixty-nine years later at Dien Bien Phu. The fort in question was called Tuyen-Kwang, situated some 100 miles north of Hanoi on the Claire river. Like Dien Bien Phu, it was so located that it was impractical to defend against a modern army, since it lay in a hollow ringed with heavily forested mountains. In short, all that the attackers had to do was to bring in enough artillery to shell it from every point of the compass. And this is what happened at Tuyen-Kwang in 1885, and at Dien Bien Phu in 1954.

(*inset*) Major Dominé, hero of the defence of the fort of Tuyen-Kwang (*below*), held off a force of some 20,000 enemy troops with the aid of two companies of the Legion. The siege was lifted after thirty-five days.

In January 1885 the Third and Fourth Companies of the Legion – 390 men and eight officers – joined the garrison of 210 French soldiers defending the fort of Tuyen-Kwang. This little force was commanded by a Major, later Colonel Marc-Edmond Dominé, one of those French officers who had devoted his life to the service of his country. He had been wounded in Africa during an Algerian campaign in April 1870 and again in December of the same year during the Franco-Prussian

The small fortress of Tuyen-Kwang was typical of the strongholds built by Chinese military engineers and then captured and manned by the French. Such forts were not really suitable for defence against a modern army, but proved adequate to hold off Indo-Chinese rebels armed only with antiquated weapons. Tuyen-Kwang was almost encircled by jungle in which the attackers could hide while they built up their forces. They then advanced stage by stage by means of lines of trenches and tunnels, some of these underground passages reaching right up to and inside the walls of the fort. The Legion relied on its siege guns (including the armament of a small gunboat in the Claire River) to keep the attackers pinned down in their trenches, though the Black Flags, estimated to number some 20,000 men, made frequent frontal assaults, only to be hurled back by the legionnaires. Tuyen-Kwang held out for thirty-five days, when a relief column came through from Hanoi.

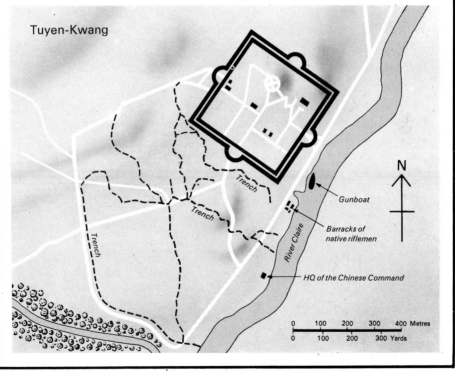

Tuyen-Kwang

N

Trench

Trench

Trench

River Claire

Gunboat

Barracks of native riflemen

HQ of the Chinese Command

| 0 | 100 | 200 | 300 | 400 Metres |
| 0 | 100 | 200 | 300 Yards | |

war. On the second occasion the surgeons had wanted to amputate
Dominé's arm, but he declared, 'My career would be ruined. I prefer to
die.' He did not die and his arm was saved, but it was almost useless and
he could salute only with difficulty. (The French army of that period
continued to keep semi-crippled men on active service, so that we find
the one-armed Captain Danjou in command of a company in Mexico
and the disabled Major Dominé in command of a garrison in Indo-
China.)

Luu-Vinh-Phuoc, the commander of the Black Flags and Chinese
regulars who were besieging Tuyen-Kwang, quickly realized that it
was useless to attack the French fort with the traditional 'do-or-die'
tactics. Instead he waited until he could place his guns overlooking the
besieged citadel, while assembling his army of some 20,000 men in the
jungle which covered the surrounding heights. Sixty-nine years later a
Vietnamese general called Giap was to use precisely the same tactics
against the fortress complex of Dien Bien Phu. Almost the only difference was that Giap had modern cannon; Luu-Vinh-Phuoc had only a
few museum pieces.

The situation inside Tuyen-Kwang was more reminiscent of a
lengthy medieval siege than of modern warfare. In fact, such a siege in
which a small force of professional European soldiers held off an enormous army of native insurgents was typical of the colonial wars of
France and Britain at the time. In the long run the advantages lay with
the besieged *provided* relief came before the food or water or ammunition ran out. The besiegers, on the other hand, had their problems,
notably the lack of siege engines powerful enough to breach the walls.

In lieu of such weapons, Phuoc had to use his almost inexhaustible
reserves of manpower. Assault columns were repeatedly sent against
the fort until the general realized that no amount of trumpet calls,
banging of gongs, or waving of huge banners would affect either the
morale or the deadly crossfire of the besieged. Nor would the discharge
of incalculable numbers of bullets – 30,000 in one day, according to one
observer – nor the propaganda shouted through the night and directed
at the loyal Tonkinese who were serving with the French. 'Surrender!
Go away! If the French don't clear off, we shall take them and cut off
their heads and raise them on stakes on the ramparts . . .'[4] Luu-Vinh-
Phuoc therefore decided to wait until all the troops he could muster –
his own Black Flag bands and several detachments of the Chinese army
sent down from the north – were in place, throwing a ring round the
fort and thus, theoretically, sealing it off from the outside world. But the

Native spies were used extensively to report on troop movements and to act as messengers called 'coolie-trams'.

theory had little to do with the practice, and in point of fact Major Dominé's garrison was at no time cut off from the main French forces at Hanoi to the south. Communications were maintained by messengers evocatively called 'coolie-trams'. These natives travelled alone either on foot through the jungle or on rafts down the rivers, all of which flowed in a south-easterly direction from the interior into the Gulf of Tonkin, and all of which were navigable for most of their length.

On 11 February 1885 a coolie-tram took an urgent message from Major Dominé to a French post at Vietri, stating that the fort was surrounded and that the Chinese were driving tunnels under the walls. The coolie-tram's chances of getting through the Chinese lines were now slim. He decided that the only way to get through was by floating down the river, but not on a raft, for the enemy was keeping watch on both banks. He solved the problem by tying loosely together a bundle of bamboo canes to look much like the other flotsam and jetsam floating downstream. He then divested himself of his clothes, rolled them into a bundle, and tied them under the bamboo sticks. Next, he slipped soundlessly into the water, keeping only his head above the surface in the middle of this tiny 'raft'. If he suspected danger he ducked under the water and breathed through a bamboo cane. In this manner, he floated and swam some forty miles down the river, to land safely at the French post at Vietri. The message he brought from Major Dominé said:

> Today I feel that I must inform you that even though the will to resist remains the same, yet our strength and health will have soon reached their limit, and I think that it is most important that a column as strong as possible be sent to raise the siege of Tuyen-Kwang.[5]

Major Dominé's anxiety was due not so much to the continuous shelling and frontal assaults of the enemy, as to the gradual approach of several tunnels up to and under the walls of the fort. This meant that in a matter of days the Chinese would be able to blow a hole in the ramparts and to rush in through the breach, overwhelming the defenders by sheer weight of numbers. One mine had already been exploded, and while the Legion was counter-attacking, a second mine went up, then a third. The danger was again averted by a bayonet charge, the legionnaires having long since discovered that native peoples were particularly terrified of cold steel. In fact, although the Black Flags with the Chinese regulars rushed into the breaches now being made every day by the continual sapping, the legionnaires were able to repel them time and again, and even to launch counter-attacks outside the fortress walls.

In general the siege of Tuyen-Kwang was typical of the time and place. The French had a handful of trained and disciplined professional soldiers, among them two companies of the Legion; the 'Celestials' (as the Chinese were called by Westerners) had a sizeable army of some 'regulars' and more 'volunteers'. These troops were employed as a substitute for heavy artillery. There was, then, always the possibility that they would triumph by sheer weight of numbers, particularly when this was combined with a fanaticism engendered by drugs, hysteria, or the threats of their commanders. There was also the possibility that the besieged would simply reach the end of their physical endurance through lack of sleep. (There was, incidentally, never any shortage of food, water, or ammunition.) But as long as these remained mere possibilities the outcome was never really in much doubt, due to the spirit of no surrender which had now become a Legion tradition. And so when thirty-five days after the siege of Tuyen-Kwang had begun the French garrison heard cannon-fire to the south-east, they knew that relief was on its way, and victory was theirs. They had saved the fortress at a cost of thirty-two killed and 126 wounded out of a total garrison of just under 600. Most of the casualties were from the Legion battalions, as usual.

By 1890 the French army had pretty well suppressed all organized military opposition throughout Tonkin which had been formally ceded to France in 1885 by the Chinese. Victory had cost them 15,000 men – the majority of whom had succumbed to disease. However, the guerilla warfare waged by the brigands continued and since fighting guerillas was the corps' speciality, learnt over several decades in the mountains and deserts of North Africa, three battalions of the Legion were kept permanently in Indo-China until the First World War. They soon became as adept at jungle warfare as they had become at desert fighting. Their life is described by the British volunteer George Manington, who tells us that the French soldiers hated the country, the army, and the expedition – with reason (he says), for they were 'town-bred, beardless boys of from eighteen to twenty years of age, and unfortunate enough to draw a low number from the conscription urn'.[6] These were the kind of lads, fresh from home, who were to die by the tens of thousands in disease-haunted places like Madagascar, Tonkin, and Cambodia. They sat by their camp fires, Manington writes, talking in subdued tones of their homes and loved ones. The legionnaire, in contrast, being a soldier of fortune, an older and more experienced man, inured to danger, hardship, and, to some extent, even disease, enjoyed the life he had chosen and, if led by an officer whose courage was undisputed, could go to meet his death with light-hearted gaiety.

At all events, Indo-China began to enjoy both peace and prosperity, and French culture (including the French language) took a profound hold on the Vietnamese townspeople. But the occupiers could never weaken, either by a benevolent or a ruthless policy, the determination of the Indo-Chinese people themselves to gain independence, so that it was inevitable that one day the struggle for independence would begin again. The siege of Tuyen-Kwang, symbolic of the initial French conquest of Indo-China, was to be repeated at Dien Bien Phu. The circumstances, geographical, military and political, were almost the same. So were the contenders. Only this time the result was different, so different that it could be said that after Dien Bien Phu the French empire, the French army, and the French Foreign Legion would never be the same again.

The Legion in the First World War

The enormity of the numbers of men engaged in the First World War, the ferocity of the battles, and the immensity of the losses in lives and equipment tend to overshadow the contributions of the Foreign Legion to the Allied cause, despite the courage and sacrifices of these élite troops. Even so, the Legion played a vital role in many of the frontal attacks against the German lines and did so with such heroism that their battle flags were constantly decorated with new honours. Some idea of the casualties suffered by the Corps in this bloodiest of world wars is seen from the figure of 31,000 legionnaires killed, wounded, or missing as the price of the battles of Vimy Ridge, the Marne, the Somme, Hangard Wood, and the great offensives along the Western Front. At the Battle of the Somme alone, over a million men died, including one out of three from the Legion's *Régiment de Marche*. The tide of war, however, began to turn when the Germans retreated under the pressure of the Allied offensive of 1918 in which the Legion played a significant role by breaking through the Hindenburg line. (*Battles in which the Legion fought are shown on the map*).

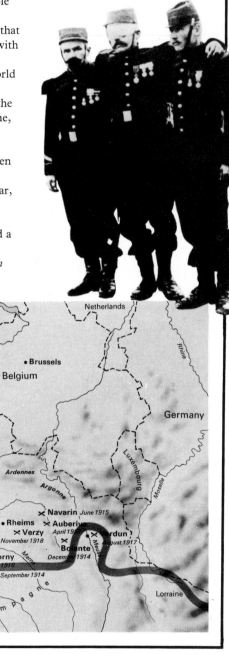

Netherlands

Rhine

Calais

• Brussels

Belgium

English Channel

Vimy Ridge ✕
April 1917

Douai
✕ *May 1915*

Germany

Somme

Bois de Hangard
April 1918 ✕

✕
Belloy-en-
Santerre
July 1916

Ardennes

Argonne

Luxembourg

Moselle

Luxembourg

Soissons
✕
✕ *May 1918*

Seine

Saint Baudry
June 1918

• Rheims

✕ Navarin *June 1915*

✕ Auberive
April 1917

✕ Verdun
August 1917

✕ Verzy
November 1918

Meuse

✕ Sorny
September 1915

Marne

✕ Bolante
December 1914

PARIS

Deepest German Penetration September 1914

Lorraine

0 20 40 60 80 Kilometres
0   20   40   60 Miles

C h a m p a g n e

The First World War 1914-18

On 4 July 1916 a foreign legionnaire named Alan Seeger died during the Battle of the Somme. This battle, which lasted 130 days, was to cost the lives of 111,000 men, 100,000 of them British, the remainder French, so that Alan Seeger's death was negligible statistically. But the character of this legionnaire and the manner of his dying were significant, first because Alan Seeger was an American who, together with 1,100 other compatriots, had volunteered for service in the Legion at the outbreak of the war; and second, because he was a poet who sacrificed his life for an ideal.

An American exile living in Paris, Alan Seeger was typical of the 'new' Foreign Legion which was quickly organized at the beginning of the First World War. 'New' because both the kind of volunteers and the regiments they formed had little in common with the now 'traditional' Legion (i.e., the First and Second Regiments) still based at Sidi-bel-Abbès. In the early days of the war the authorities were inundated with enthusiasts wanting to join the famous corps, and no doubt the professionals found them something of a nuisance. But the High Command very quickly came to realize that every man who could walk and see, irrespective of his age or physique, was needed in a war which was killing soldiers off at the rate of thousands a day – two million of them, German and Allied, dying between February and November of 1916.

And so the 44,150 foreigners who eventually served in the Legion between 1914 and 1918 were certainly welcome, and that they proved their worth as frontline soldiers was shown by their casualties – 31,000 legionnaires killed, wounded, or missing. They came from a hundred and one countries, including the enemy countries of Austro-Hungary, Germany, and Turkey. The position regarding the Germans was somewhat awkward at a time when patriotism meant not listening to Beethoven's music, but as far as the army was concerned the German legionnaires had always been the best fighters and, indeed, they were to prove so again. The most decorated non-commissioned officer in the entire French army, Sergeant-Major Mader, was a German legionnaire.

All volunteers were acceptable, though not, it should be added, to the old legionnaires who had fought in the colonial wars. For these men the

Legion was a special sort of home, as well as an élite military unit, and they tended to be sceptical of volunteers who talked about the honour of France and the need to save civilization from a new invasion by the Huns.

But the invasion of Belgium and the threat to France had aroused deep emotions in the foreigners resident in Paris, as we can judge from

The Legion received more decorations than any other unit in the First World War. Colonel Rollet (*centre*) became known as the 'Father of the Legion'.

Many Americans living in France in 1914 joined
the Foreign Legion, among them the young poet
Alan Seeger (*inset*), who died on the Western
Front.

the appeals which they sent out through their societies and associations.
The Jews, for instance, sent the following letter to all their co-religionists
in both French and Hebrew.

Brothers!
France, land of liberty, equality and fraternity; France which has liberated
mankind; France which first among all nations, has recognized on behalf
of us Jews our rights as men and citizens; France, where we have found
over many years a refuge and a home – France is in danger! And we
foreign Jews, what are we going to do? Cross our arms while the people of
France rise like one man to defend their country?

No, for even if we are not yet French by right, we are French in our
hearts and souls, and our most sacred duty is to put ourselves at the dis-
position of this great and noble nation in order to take part in its defence.
Brothers! Foreign Jews! Do your duty and long live France![1]

The British colony in Paris received a much more formal appeal, a
circular in English which called a meeting, stated the purpose ('Object:
Formation of a British Volunteer Corps, to offer its services to the French
War Minister'), and only let itself go to the extent of declaring that 'Aid-
ing our friends at such a time is the best way of serving our dear Mother
Country.'[2] The Americans, in contrast, were addressed in French by
their committee of the Friends of France, and many references were

Joffre, French Commander-in-Chief, with President Poincaré (*light uniform*) at the Front. (*left*) Underground quarters of the garrison at Verdun.

made to La Fayette and one to '*la barbarie du sabre teutonique*'. The appeal ended with '*Vive la France immortelle ! Vive la colonie américaine !*'[3]

Certainly the number and calibre of the volunteers at first created a problem for the French War Ministry, since it was not apparent how these civilians were to be incorporated into, of all units, a tough outfit like the Foreign Legion. The problem was further complicated by the lack of regular non-commissioned officers for training the recruits, since these regulars were, and always had been, preponderantly Germans. Naturally Germans were now suspect, and for this reason the two original regiments of the Legion were, for the time being, kept on duty in Algeria or Morocco. But the volunteers had to be housed and trained somehow, first in barracks at Rouen, then at Toulouse. The training was left to a colonel in the *gendarmerie* with the help of the local firemen; and eventually from this motley collection of foreigners, aged from eighteen to fifty-five, most of whom had never held a rifle before, there was formed the Third Regiment of the Foreign Legion. At the same time, some 6,000 Italians, responding to the appeal of the son and grandson of Garibaldi, were formed into a Fourth Regiment under the aegis of the Legion. They were almost immediately thrown into battle on the Argonne and almost immediately sacrificed in the now standard procedure of frontal attacks against German machine-gun posts. What was left of the Italian regiment was disbanded in May 1916 in order that the Garibaldeans could join their own army now that Italy was at war.

By November 1915, all that was left of the Third Regiment of elderly foreigners and the Fourth or Italian Regiment was incorporated into the regular Legion, whose two famous regiments, the First and the Second, had now been brought over from Africa to add their special assault skills to Marshal Joffre's campaign. Joffre belonged to an already antiquated military school which had learnt its strategy and tactics in the nineteenth-century colonial wars of Africa and Indo-China. He, together with all the other generals for that matter, continued throughout the war to order whole divisions of infantry to advance against impregnable positions. In these assaults, which required either an irrational courage or an iron discipline, the Foreign Legion was unexcelled. We find the re-formed *Régiments de Marche*, that is, regiments composed of units from Legion battalions, used by Joffre and later by Marshal Foch to carry out the more difficult assaults along the western front.

In 1915, at Vimy Ridge, six corps of the French army with one corps in reserve prepared for the attack. The Moroccan Division in the centre, including four battalions of the Legion, was assigned to take a vital strongpoint called Hill 140. At precisely two minutes to ten on the morning of 9 May, the artillery bombardment stopped and the officers of the First and Second Battalions of the Foreign Legion, like the officers of other battalions all along the line, synchronized their watches, then gave the command, with cries or whistles, to go over the top. (The Legion, incidentally, continued to use the trumpet to signal its battle orders, and the spectacle of the Legion 'bugler' standing up in the midst of a hail of machine-gun-bullets and trumpeting the officer's command to advance was one of the few romantic sights of the trench warfare.) And so the First and Second Battalions set off to attack Hill 140. Their reception as they ran across No Man's Land was to become standard in all these massed attacks of the war. Despite a week's continuous bombardment a number of the enemy's concrete pill-boxes were still standing, while the enemy troops in the forward trenches, who had retired by transverse escape routes during the barrage, had been brought back to key positions as soon as the artillery stopped. Thus the legionnaires, the Moroccan, British, and French divisions, along the entire eight miles of the front were met by a withering cross fire and died by the tens of thousands. The legionnaires, trained to advance against North African strongholds on mountain summits, and superbly led by professional soldiers, fared better than most units. They took cover where it was available, spotted those corridors which were not enfiladed by machine-gun fire, advanced round and behind pill-boxes, and quickly gained the comparative safety of the enemy's trenches before the German artillery opened up in a counter-barrage.

The extraordinary thing was that the Legion, despite its losses, did finally fight its way to the summit of Hill 140, while the Moroccan division, commanded by General Ernest-Joseph Blondlat, also attained its objectives, though at an appalling cost in lives. General Blondlat telephoned the news to corps headquarters: the breakthrough was now possible, provided fresh troops could be thrown into the breach made by the legionnaires and the Zouaves. The enemy seemed to be in confusion as he retreated. This was the time to exploit the initial victory. Unfortunately for the victors, a characteristic muddle behind the lines caused a long delay in sending up reinforcements. The Moroccan division and the Legion battalion holding Hill 140 were ordered to withdraw. They did so with almost as much danger and difficulty as they had encountered in advancing. The dead included all three battalion commanders. The colonel of the Regiment, Jacques Pein, had only been in command for a day when he received a mortal wound 'on the field of honour'. Once again a Legion unit had been practically wiped out in a single battle.

Within three months it was re-formed and committed to the Champagne offensive. Marshal Joffre still believed that frontal attacks on the German positions, if on a large enough scale, would achieve the necessary breakthrough. By 25 September, after the usual prolonged artillery bombardment, Joffre gave the order to attack with two entire French armies massed along a fifteen-mile front between Rheims and Verdun. So sanguine were the French High Command that they had squadrons of cavalry and fleets of buses ready to dash through the breaches to be made in the German lines. And, as a special aid to victory, clouds of mustard gas were formed over the enemy positions.

There was, of course, no breakthrough and no change whatsoever in the fortunes of war. The Legion, which had been thrown into the attack on 27 September had fought with its usual *panache*, even to the extent of having its bugler play the regimental hymn, *Le Boudin*, during the advance across No Man's Land. But the sound of a trumpet could not stop machine-gun bullets, and advancing legionnaires fell dead or wounded by the hundreds. Survivors of the battle tell how a number of men stripped off their uniforms in an attempt to break loose from the

French decorations. (*above left*) *Légion d'Honneur* (*right*) *Médaille Militaire*. (*below*) The three *Croix de Guerre*: overseas, 1939–45, and 1914–18.

A French '155' at Verdun. Both sides used enormous cannon to pulverize the enemy in their trenches and fortifications along the Western Front.

entangling wire, only to be shot dead by snipers as they revealed their white undershirts. At all events, the 1,500 legionnaires were reduced within a few hours to 800. The offensive was broken off on 28 September, with nothing achieved.

The story of the subsequent First World War battles are well documented. The Legion's role on the Western Front (*see map page 80*) involved the usual heavy losses. At the Battle of the Somme (1916), 1,264,105 men died (one of them Alan Seeger) roughly half of them Allies, half German. In a battle on this scale, in which eighteen British divisions and five French divisions faced eleven German divisions, the Legion's *Régiment de Marche* consisting of 2,500 legionnaires could play only a minute part. They played it with their usual skill and brilliance, capturing the village of Belloy-en-Santerre where twenty-five officers and 844 men died and were buried in the military cemetery nearby. The remains of Alan Seeger were never found, although his father came from America hoping to find his dead son and to take him home. There is no tombstone commemorating Corporal Seeger (1888–1916) of the Second Regiment of the Foreign Legion, but he can still speak to us through his poems:

> And on those furthest rims of hallowed ground
> Where the forlorn, the gallant charge expires,
> When the slain bugler has long ceased to sound,
> And on tangled wires
> The last wild rally staggers, crumbles, stops,
> Withered beneath the shrapnel's iron showers:—
> Now heaven be thanked, we gave a few brave drops;
> Now heaven be thanked, a few brave drops were ours.[1]

It could be said that these lines summed up the nobility as well as the horror of the First World War and described in a few perfect phrases a typical Legion attack whether on the battlefields of Europe, in the African desert, or in the jungles of Asia.

(*right*) An ambulance car used on the light railway at Verdun. (*below*) Dressing-stations, like this one in the casemates of a French fort, were hardpressed by the constant stream of casualties brought in from the front lines.

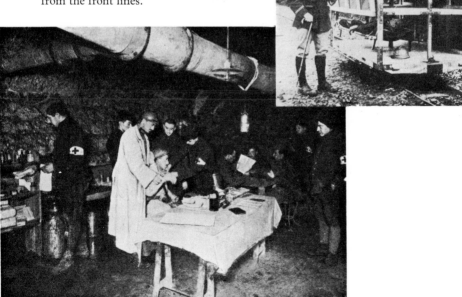

The Legion in Morocco

The conquest and pacification of Morocco were made
possible largely by the efforts of the Legion, since this
formidable country of mountain ranges, deserts, and fiercely
independent people entailed a type of combat for which the
Legion had been trained in the Algerian wars. While the
regular French army was able to hold the large coastal cities
like Rabat and Casablanca and to keep control of centres of
population in the interior (Fez, Khenifra, Marrakesh), peace
was constantly threatened by the warlike Berber tribes of the
Rif and Atlas Mountains. The Legion's role was to contain
the insurgents by establishing and garrisoning a chain of
forts through the long valleys in order to keep open
communications with Algeria to the east. When Abd el-Krim
united the Moroccans in a national uprising, however, the
French needed a full-size army to cope with the rebellion.
Even so, the Legion still formed the spearhead of the
assaults on the mountain strongholds where, after the defeat
of el-Krim, other Berber leaders held out in the Djebel
Baddou region of the High Atlas, until they were starved
into submission in 1933. As a French protectorate until the
country was granted full independence in 1939, Morocco
had six years of peace and progress; and today an excellent
network of roads – largely built by French military
engineers with the help of battalions of the Legion – links
cities like Fez and Meknès and the southern oases of
Tafilelt and Tiznit to the capital Rabat.

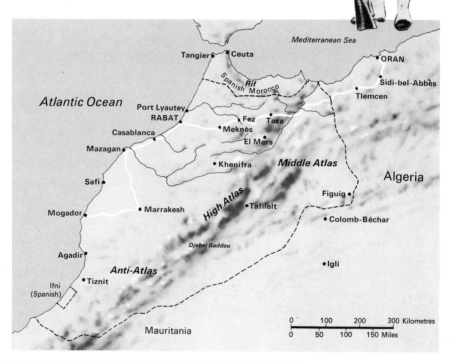

Morocco 1900-39 · Syria 1925-6

Morocco

After the First World War the French were occupied with the formidable task of policing 322,000 square miles of Morocco, which had been more or less a protectorate of France since 1880. During the hostilities in Europe, this task had been left to Marshal Lyautey, perhaps their greatest colonial general and administrator. But Lyautey had insufficient men for the job and now relied almost wholly on the Legion to control those regions of the country which were, superficially, pacified. The Legion's role, therefore, was to build and garrison forts in strategic places, to link these strongholds with roads, and to quell rebellion wherever it broke out. A British legionnaire described an attack on a French fort in southern Morocco which was typical of hundreds of such skirmishes during the Berber uprising of 1925 to 1926 led by Abd el-Krim.

I must have dozed for a bit, for I suddenly woke with a start to hear a shrill cry like a child screaming with pain, then a volley of rifle shots rent the air, followed by the well-known shout of '*Illa illa allah akbar*'. I leapt to my feet as I heard the sous-officer crying '*Aux armes! Aux armes! Prenez la garde, Légionnaires.*' Then I heard a blood-curdling yell and I knew the sentries had been shot . . . Men were crying out as they fell pierced by knife or bullet. A fierce hand to hand fight was now in progress on the top of the bastions. My friend Dell [a Canadian], the one man in the Legion I cared for had been cut up right from the chest, and his eyes were staring with a pitiful look of surprise on his deadly white face. One hand was on his rifle but the other had been shot away.

Seeing the dark faces of the Arabs in front of me and knowing it was they who had knifed my pal, I went berserk and fought like a madman . . . from another part of the fort we could hear the sharp rat tat of the machine guns pouring their deadly spray of bullets into the black mass of Arabs outside. But where we were, they could not be used, as the enemy were right in the middle of us. I advanced to within a few feet of the Captain standing on top of the wall. He seemed madder than ever, and now and again he roared with laughter. Then he broke into wild shouting, crying '*Allez*, you swine of Morocco. *En avant la Légion. Vive la Légion.*'

He emptied his revolver into the thick of the fight, not seeming to care whether he hit his own men or the Arabs; so long as he shot someone. He was standing on the edge of the wall and suddenly with one last wild cry of '*Vive la Légion*' I saw him topple over backwards and disappear.[1]

The ferocious courage of the captain seems to have been characteristic of Legion commanders from the very first engagements of the corps in the 1830s. To Prince Aage of Denmark, even the battles in which the legionnaires and Berbers cut each other to pieces with knives and bayonets were 'beautiful'.

> That was a beautiful assault. We advanced slowly in small groups, saving our breath for the bayonet work . . . Men were dropping in scores; it seemed as if the distance to the trenches would never diminish. Then, setting itself, the Legion rushed . . . It was bloody work. The tribesmen, cut off from any possible assistance, flatly refused to surrender. Throwing their rifles down, they drew their long knives and sold their lives as dearly as possible.[2]

Even the atrocities and brutalities of this unpopular war (that is, unpopular throughout the western world, including France itself) were accepted by the Legion as part of their life. Another British legionnaire, John H. Harvey, *alias* Barrington, *alias* Ex-Legionnaire 1,384, relates how two soldiers from the Moroccan fort of Bab Mezab, which a company of the Legion was defending against the Riff, were caught by the Berbers outside the walls and buried alive in two vertical graves, with just their heads above ground.

> We watched the Riffs approach those two heads. We saw them pour over the heads a brown sticky substance, which soon we knew to be honey, for in a moment the two heads were covered with a cloud of flies, mosquitoes, scorpions, and other torturous insects. [One notes that scorpions would not normally run over a sticky substance; nor are they insects. JW.] We heard the inhuman screams that came from those heads, screams that could not be drowned even by the wild yells of the Riffs.

Harvey then tells us that his American friend, McCann, ordered by the Legion captain Dupont to put an end to his comrades' sufferings, 'took aim in the coolest manner imaginable . . . His rifle cracked. A shower of insects shot up into the air. A head lolled forward, blood streaming from the eyes. Crack! The other head shuddered!'[3]

One gains from this an idea of the type of fighting that the Legion was engaged in during almost forty years of conquering and trying to pacify Morocco. Certainly the French would never have succeeded without the final intervention of all four regiments of the Foreign Legion plus their newly-formed cavalry troop. The cavalry were, of course, the glamour unit, but it was still the infantry, and especially the Mounted Companies (two men to a mule, taking it turn and turn about to ride) who really

---

The French attacked Figuig (on the Algerian–Moroccan border) in 1903 after the Governor-General, M. Jonnart, was fired on by the Sultan's troops.

held on until the French government decided to send Marshal Pétain with an adequate army to relieve Lyautey and the hard-pressed Legion.

The appearance on the scene of a nationalist leader of real stature had finally decided Paris to act. Abd el-Krim, the Riff tribal chieftain, had, with only a few thousand warriors, almost driven the Spanish army of 19,000 men out of what was Spanish Morocco. By 1925 he was prepared to try the same tactics with the French. For a while he succeeded, attacking and seizing the Legion's forts. He even began to think in terms of a large national army, modelled on the lines of the European armies, with chiefs-of-staff, headquarters, an officer hierarchy, disciplined troops, and the machines of modern war. He was encouraged in these dreams by various European mercenaries and by a sympathetic British and American press whose journalists, with a complete miscomprehension of the nature and aims of el-Krim, reported his successes as the victories of a great patriot over a cruel occupation. There was talk of his governing Morocco according to the best western democratic principles once he had driven out the French. It was even envisaged that he might do so with the aid of his European military advisers, one of whom, a German called Joseph Klems *alias* Hadj Aleman (the German Pilgrim), was a deserter from the Legion. (Indeed, there was quite a number of deserters from the Legion at this time, largely because the chances of escaping were better in Morocco than they had ever been in Algeria. The Englishman 'Ex-Legionnaire 73,645' was able to evade the authorities quite easily, taking with him an entire squadron of Cossack cavalry, together with their horses and arms, including machine-guns. These men joined the guerillas, hiding out in a Berber village high in the Atlas Mountains, married native girls, and lived as bandits until they had to make their way to the coast to escape the French army and Legion vengeance.[4])

But in the end, all that Abd el-Krim and the other Moorish insurgents could muster against the French army were their fanatical warriors, the arms they had captured from the Spanish and the French, their hatred of the infidel invader, and the sympathy of the native population. El-Krim was supposed to have an air force but, like his liberation government, this existed largely in the minds of the pro-Berber European press.

Against him marched Marshal Pétain's new army, with all four regiments of the Legion in the vanguard. This army was something new in

Berbers, galloping along the sands at Agadir in Morocco, have changed little in appearance from the horsemen who once harassed the Legion's infantry columns.

French column entering camp, the Moroccan campaign 1907–12. (*inset left*) Marshal Lyautey, creator of French Morocco, was succeeded by Pétain (*right*).

colonial warfare. It was large and numerous enough to encircle an entire region. It was highly professional and well led. It was assisted by the sophisticated machines of modern warfare, aeroplanes, tanks, guns, radio. Nothing was overlooked, as had so often happened in previous colonial campaigns. Even the *Bordel Militaire de Campagne*, or mobile brothel, had its set place in the column and its fixed hours of opening, when a dozen or so Moroccan girls, aged between fifteen and eighteen, were visited by scores of men every night.

A veteran of the Moroccan campaign describes these prostitutes, ten or twelve Mauresques and 'a European woman who had reached the last degree of decadence', as being 'exposed to the fury of 5,000 solid young males, bubbling over with ardour and vitality'.[5] The women, who rode in motorized caravans when the column was on the move, set up tents at the end of the day and were protected on pay nights by armed guards.

Abd el-Krim led the Riffian revolt against both the Spanish and French occupations. His headquarters in the mountains were often bombed from the air.

Inter-regimental fights were avoided by appointing particular days to particular regiments. Such mobile brothels became a standard feature of all French colonial armies.

The last act in the long drama of Morocco took place in the High Atlas in the Spring of 1933. Abd el-Krim had been utterly defeated and surrendered in May 1926, and nearly every cell of resistance throughout the country had been wiped out, largely by the use of the Legion. But the spirit of rebellion lingered on in the villages of the High Atlas. Here other Berber leaders, all sharing the same fanatical hatred of the French, took up arms against the occupiers and fought it out from their mountain strongholds.

One of these natural fortresses was the Djebel Baddou, and here a chieftain called Ouskounti prepared to defy with 2,000 warriors a modern army of 25,000 men. It was intended to be a fight to the death, for the rebel position was regarded as impregnable even by some of the French intelligence officers. They pointed out that neither ground shelling nor aerial bombing could reach the rebels inside their caves. Nor, it was assumed, could the infantry, who were not, after all, *alpinistes*. None the less, General Giraud gave the order to attack, probably because it would have appeared somewhat ridiculous to assemble an army of such strength and size and not to use it. And so, after an artillery and air bombardment which was more impressive to the attackers in the foothills than the attacked in their grottoes, two columns proceeded to climb the 6,500 foot peaks, one consisting of the so-called partisans, that is, Moroccans who were now fighting as mercenaries for the French; the other consisting of the Mounted Company of the Second Regiment of the Legion. The Moroccans were led by the famous Captain Henri de Lespinasse de Bournazel, who went into battle in an immaculate scarlet uniform, armed only with a riding-whip. His indifference to death and danger was such that a legend circulated among the Berbers that he was invulnerable, until, that is, a sharpshooter picked him off as he marched at the head of his company, followed by his standard-bearer. He fell mortally wounded, aged thirty-five; his soldiers wavered and eventually fled. And so it was left to the Legion to continue the assault. It was done in the now traditional heroic style. The officers were the first to die, as Captain de Bournazel had died at the head of his troops. So Lieutenant Brenklé of the Second Regiment was mortally wounded, and four of his platoon, his sergeant-major, sergeant, and two legionnaires were killed soon after as they hurled their grenades at the Berbers firing from behind a natural parapet of rocks. Next, Captain Fauchaux, scorning to run in a crouching posture from one position to another, was hit as he walked upright across the field of fire. This left two lieutenants and a handful of legionnaires to attempt to capture a crest despite a rain of bullets from the Berbers who were well placed behind boulders and hidden in crevices among the rocks. Lieutenant Binet fell dead with three bullet wounds. The remaining officer and twelve men were all that got back safely after the attack had been called off as ineffectual.

Yet this sacrifice of élite soldiers was unnecessary, since the French were now in a position to hold the wells or to interdict them by artillery fire. Ouskounti, his warriors, their wives and children, their herds and their flocks, were all doomed to die of thirst unless they could obtain water. The women, crouching in caves whose roofs sometimes collapsed on them as a daring French pilot managed to skim a bomb into the mouth of the cavern, had no milk with which to feed their babies, who were

Berber villagers in the Grand Atlas watch from their rooftops as the French occupy another centre of resistance.

dying of thirst. When the Berbers tried to break out and make for the water sources, the French annihilated both them and their animals. After six weeks the rebel chief surrendered. The Moroccan war of pacification was over. It had lasted nearly forty years and cost an estimated 100,000 dead.

Syria

Concurrently with the post-war French attempts to pacify Morocco, detachments of the Legion were fighting a nationalist uprising in Syria, in this case against another fanatically religious Moslem tribe, similar in their life-style to the Riffs, namely, the Druse of Syria and the Lebanon. These fierce and independent people, whose religion bade them despise all infidels, notably the Christians, were encouraged by the success of Abd el-Krim and proceeded in 1925 to mount a holy war against the occupiers of their lands. At first the tribesmen were supported by nationalists all over Syria, notably the newly formed Peoples Party, and the combined forces of the insurgents had considerable success against the small French military units sent against them. In fact, the Syrians virtually annihilated a French column sent to the relief of the town of Salkhad and then defeated a second and stronger column. These victories encouraged them in the winter of 1925 to attempt to drive the French out altogether. But the Druse from the mountains and the nationalists from the towns had no suitable weapons with which to destroy the French planes and tanks brought in to assist the Legion. As a result, the rebellion lasted for only eighteen months, for the Druse tribesmen were never properly organized or led, nor did they have the geographical advantages of the Riffians. Indeed, their only tactics consisted of attacking *en masse*, as at Messifre and Rachaya, two insignificant villages defended by a battalion of the Legion against 3,000 enemy. The Syrian warriors sacrificed themselves by the hundreds against machine-guns and bayonets, 1,000 of them being killed or wounded in a two-day battle at Messifre where the Legion losses were forty-seven killed and eighty-three wounded. Two items from the commanders' subsequent reports are characteristic of the Legion's laconic style. From Captain Boissier of the First Legion Regiment at Messifre:

> During the morning a number of attacks were repulsed by the legionnaires who fired as calmly as if on a firing-range. One saw the enemy mown down in entire groups. In front of Post A, a solitary horseman who had managed to survive our fire jumped the barbed wire and was shot dead, he and his horse together, at the foot of the wall.[6]

and from Lieutenant Medrano of the First Cavalry Regiment, who took command at Rachaya when his captain was killed:

> The last carrier pigeon was sent off with a description of the state of affairs and an urgent demand for help. It was also stressed that if help failed to arrive, an attempt would be made to save the maximum number of men by fighting a way through the encircling enemy lines at the point of the bayonet.[7]

But in this case help did arrive in the form of a French air attack on the Syrian rebels, and the Legion garrison was relieved.

Yet despite continual defeats in a series of minor engagements, the tribesmen continued to harass the French occupation forces wherever they could. The Legion was continually in pursuit, employing the tactics which they had learnt in Algeria and Morocco, occupying hostile villages, punishing the inhabitants by cutting down their fruit trees, then marching on again to deal with the enemy in a new trouble spot.

Finally, by the autumn of 1926, the French High Command decided to crush the rebellion by assigning the air force to bomb those towns and villages reported to be sympathetic to the rebels. When Damascus itself joined in the revolt, it, too, was bombed and over a thousand of its inhabitants killed. The uprising ended in 1927 when the Druse tribesmen withdrew to their mountains, after which the policing of the territory was left to detachments of the Legion who remained in Syria until the Second World War. With the independence of Syria in 1941, the Legion was withdrawn and sent back to headquarters at Sidi-bel-Abbès.

The attack by the Druse tribesmen on a Legion force defending the military post at Messifre in Syria was typical of the French colonial wars of the second half of the nineteenth and the first half of the twentieth centuries. French strategy was to hold key strongpoints controlling the surrounding countryside, and the Legion was usually given the more dangerous assignments of this sort. But once secure inside, the garrison was usually able to repulse the prolonged attacks of the most ferocious warriors, thanks to their superior arms and superb discipline. Their role was to hold out, no matter what the cost, until a relief column came through. And in the case of Messifre, the legionnaires were able to withstand the continuous attacks of the tribesmen, though with heavy losses. The defence by a small unit of the Legion of Messifre and another Syrian village called Rachaya against thousands of the enemy can be compared with the siege at Camerone in 1863 and Tuyen-Kwang in 1885 (*see chapters 5 and 7*). The strategy of colonial wars changed radically in the second half of the twentieth century as the nationalists acquired modern armaments. Isolated forts were no longer impregnable even when defended by the Legion.

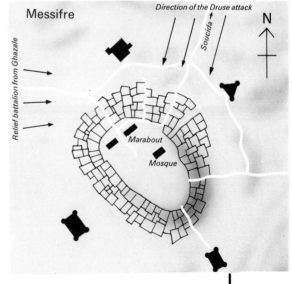

The Legion, which began the Second World War in its historic role as regiments of élite foreign troops in the service of the French army, ended by being absorbed into various Allied units in Europe, Africa, and the Middle East. Detachments of the Legion fought with the British Eighth Army in Libya (Bir Hakeim) and Egypt (El Alamein); others were assigned to the American divisions in North Africa and Italy. At the same time, those legionnaires who supported General de Gaulle joined the Free French; those who did not, returned to their bases in Africa and gave their allegiance to the Vichy régime. The result was that the Legion was scattered throughout the theatre of war from Britain to Indo-China, fighting for the Allied cause on three continents; but it was no longer one unified and easily identifiable corps known as *La Légion Etrangère*. Once the war was over, the Legion resumed its traditional role at its old headquarters in Algeria.

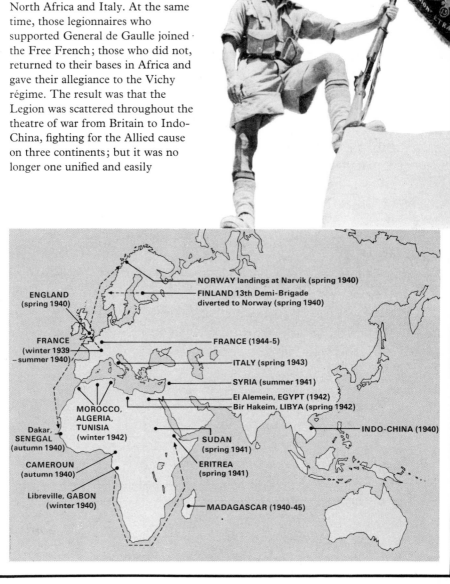

The Second World War 1939-45

Just as the First World War, with its huge armies, prolonged artillery duels, and massed assaults, was not suited to the Legion's brand of fighting, so the second of these international conflicts was far too complex for its outcome to be affected by the participation of a few regiments of foreign mercenaries. In fact, there was now something positively old-fashioned and even comic about a military unit which set off to a mid-twentieth century war accompanied by its mules and its mobile brothel, which is how a Legion brigade crossed to Marseilles in March 1940. Moreover, political factors now made the very existence of a Foreign Legion questionable. To whom, for instance, was a band of mercenaries, largely sub-officered by Germans, known to be infiltrated by Nazis, and later under the control of the Vichy government, to whom was this Legion supposed to be loyal?

Yet the need for trained fighters and, above all, the need for expendable soldiers, was a pressing concern. In 1940, for instance, help had been promised to Finland in that country's resistance to the Russian invasion. The remnants of the Legion which had been fighting in France from 1939 to 1940 were now given this hopeless assignment – hopeless because it quickly became evident that the convoys taking them to the Finnish front had little chance of successfully running the German blockade through the Skagerrak and across the Baltic. In the meantime, the Germans had invaded Norway, and so it was decided to divert units of the Legion assigned to Finland to attack Narvik in Norway. But even though they succeeded in capturing the German stronghold, they had to be withdrawn immediately afterwards in order to help the French divisions attempting to hold the German drive to the French Channel ports. By now, however, it was too late. The French armies had collapsed, their government was on the point of surrender, and what was left of the defeated French and British troops, including detachments of the Legion, made their way, by what means they could to England.

One can see, then, that in the midst of these disasters the survival of the Foreign Legion was of no particular importance to the politicians who, in 1940, were more responsible for the overall direction of the war than the generals whose armies were defeated. Who were these troops?

The Foreign Legion? They represented almost every known nationality and, it was suspected, were infiltrated with traitors and spies. At the beginning of the war, their ranks had been swollen by thousands of volunteers living in France – Jews, Russians, anti-nazis, anti-fascists, and, once again, idealists like Alan Seeger. The question was were these volunteers any use as soldiers? For their part, the veteran legionnaires of the African-based regiments very much doubted it. They felt that the old Legion was about to lose its identity. The invaluable *esprit de corps* seemed to be diminished; the famous *mystique* was threatened.

The resultant confusion about the role of the Legion and, indeed, of its actual loyalty to the Allies was demonstrated on 30 June 1940 when the so-called Thirteenth Demi-Brigade lined up in a field near Stoke-on-Trent to be addressed by General Charles de Gaulle. The general made the issue perfectly clear: there were now two nations called France, one a vassal of the Germans; the other Free France. The legionnaires had a choice: which France did they want to serve? Their colonel, Marie-Pierre Koenig, and about half of his men elected to join de Gaulle as 'Free Frenchmen'; the others, mostly Germans and Italians, decided to return to Morocco.

And so the Legion did survive but under various formations and nomenclatures: at one time as the Thirteenth Demi-Brigade, at another the Fourteenth Demi-Brigade, at another the *Régiment Etranger d'Infanterie de Marche*, at another the *Groupe Autonome*, and so on. The old Legion, the Legion of Algeria and Morocco, remained in Africa, and gave its allegiance to Vichy. Inevitably, because of the political divisions among the French, *two* Legions were to come face to face as enemies in West Africa, at Dakar in Senegal, and again at Libreville in Gabon. In Syria the Sixth Regiment under General Dentz, a Vichy man, and the Thirteenth Demi-Brigade under General Monclar, a Free Frenchman, actually met in combat; the notion of allegiance to the Legion above all else was, for the time being at least, outmoded.

So, in a sense, the Legion had almost disappeared as an individual and independent unit, the proudest and most decorated unit of the French army; and what remained of it became absorbed piecemeal into the khaki-clad, steel-helmeted formations of the Anglo-American military establishment. Legionnaires fought with other Free Frenchmen at Bir Hakeim in Libya during the great Rommel offensive of May 1942 which was temporarily halted by the resistance at Tobruk, defended by Australian troops, and, forty miles to the south in the full desert, at Bir Hakeim, defended by the French. Among the 5,500 French troops commanded by General Koenig at Bir Hakeim, were two battalions of the Legion. The remainder were mostly colonial troops. They held out against continuous Italian and German attacks supported by tanks, guns, and bombers for fifteen days, without any outside help except from the R.A.F. Ammunition, food, and, above all, water were practically finished when the order came from the British High Command to evacuate Bir Hakeim, which was done in the course of the night of 10 June. General Koenig was driven out in his jeep by the only woman ever known to have served in the Foreign Legion, Miss Susan Travers.

Not altogether surprisingly, the French felt bitter about Bir Hakeim, even though the British credited them with a victory since they had helped to hold up Rommel's projected invasion of Egypt. But the French commanders felt that their troops were being neglected, not provided with proper arms and vehicles, and, more sinister (according, that is, to the French commentators), were being used for the most dangerous assignments. Such an assignment, it is said, was given the Legion in 1942 by Montgomery at El Alamein, 'a mission that one rarely reserves for one's best friends'.[1] The Thirteenth Demi-Brigade (as the Legion was still called) was given the southernmost sector of the

(*left*) Free French gunners defend Bir Hakeim during Rommel's offensive in the Western Desert. (*below*) Legionnaires, wearing their white kepis in preference to steel helmets, rush an enemy strongpoint.

El Alamein line where it was ordered to create a diversion by attacking
a very strong German position on the other side of a ravine. It was to be
a typical Legion frontal assault, an infantry charge across open ground
'into the jaws of death'. This time the Legion was really stopped short
in its heroic charge; its men died uselessly, and another of its most
admired and loved commanders was killed. He was Prince Dimitri
Amilakvari, a Georgian noble, cadet of Saint-Cyr, posted at his own
request to the Legion in Morocco, captain of a company on the Narvik
raid, a hero of Bir Hakeim, killed, aged thirty-six, at El Alamein. His
manner of living, fighting, and dying was the acme of the Legion officers'
code; he would go into battle impeccably turned out, right down to the
swagger-stick, for, as he is credited with saying, 'a man should go
before his Maker properly dressed'.

But the *beau geste* of Lieutenant-Colonel Prince Amilakvari was lost
on or ignored by a world in which whole continents were being fought
over and entire armies were being liquidated. New élite formations –
the commandos, paratroops, Desert Rats, and so on – were making
the headlines. One cannot recall any mention of the Foreign Legion in
the despatches of the British and American war correspondents, for by
1942 the corps had been completely absorbed into the two major armies,
British and American. Thus the Thirteenth Demi-Brigade was now an
integral part of the Eighth Army, its officers and men indistinguishable
in their uniforms and procedures from any British brigade. The 'old'
Legion, namely, those units which had stayed in North Africa or had
elected to go there and serve Marshal Pétain in preference tó General
de Gaulle, had been absorbed into the American army after the Anglo-
American invasion of North Africa in 1942.

There were still to be occasions, however, when the Allied Commanders needed the super-heroic soldiers traditionally provided by the
Legion, as in 1943 during the war in Italy when a squad of six legionnaires captured the castle of Radocofani on the old road between Rome
and Florence. Situated high on a precipitous rock, the castle was
defended at the base by three Tiger tanks and within the walls by a
company of German infantrymen. A section of the legionnaires attacked
the tanks while others climbed the rock and took the castle from the
rear, using the Legion's favourite weapon, the hand grenade. This was
the kind of warfare for which the Legion had been renowned.

A typical makeshift cookhouse in the front line manned by legionnaires: one
man prepares *la soupe*; another scrounges enough hot water to shave.

Indo-China 1946-54

Of all the chapters in Legion history, Indo-China proved the most tragic, ending with the almost apocalyptic disaster of Dien Bien Phu. The tragedy is reflected in the Legion casualty list for those eight years: 10,482 killed in action; more than 30,000 wounded; 2,567 survivors out of 6,328 prisoners of war. Total: nearly 45,000 legionnaires sacrificed in a cruel, hopeless, and unjustifiable war.

It did not seem hopeless, of course, when the French came back to Indo-China in 1946, after the Japanese had withdrawn. Admittedly the army commanders and civilian administrators who returned were not too happy at what they found. Five thousand men of the Fifth Regiment of the Legion left in Indo-China to police that territory had disappeared during the Japanese occupation; and without the Legion, control of the countryside was virtually impossible.

More alarming, however, to the returning French were the political forces which had filled the vacuum left by the defeated occupiers. The Vietminh no more wanted to be ruled by the French than they had been by the Japanese, and opposition to the new French occupation began at once in 1946. It soon became obvious that the best hope of keeping the peace in Indo-China lay in the fighting abilities of the Foreign Legion which had been the principal instrument in pacifying Morocco after the First World War.

Accordingly, the French War Ministry redoubled its efforts at recruitment, even welcoming into the Legion fugitive Nazis and Fascists who were only too eager to lose their identity and at the same time pursue the only way of life they knew – professional soldiering. (One of these volunteers was a German parachute officer who had rescued Mussolini in the Abruzzi in 1944.) It is estimated that the Legion, now sixty per cent German, was built up to a complement of some 10,000 men. Their task, however, was formidable. First, they were fighting, in the initial stages of the campaign, a secret army. Second, they were fighting in swamps and jungles. And third, there were not enough legionnaires

Aerial view of Dien Bien Phu, and the vital airfield by which the besieged fortress maintained contact with the outside world for five months.

to occupy and police those districts which were nominally conquered and pacified. The war, therefore, was unpredictable, arduous, and apparently unending.

The type of warfare the Legion was involved in during the early period (1946–60) is well described by the English legionnaire, Henry Ainley.[1] There were frequent raids on Vietminh outposts in forests, swamps, and mountains; reprisals against villages suspected of harbouring enemies of the French régime; and long marches across roadless country to relieve beleaguered forts. Under these conditions, where squads of men were confined for months at a time in jungle outposts, alcohol was obviously an easy panacea; and when he was not on duty, and sometimes even when he was, the legionnaire was tempted to forget his troubles by drinking. The authorities, in fact, recognized the need for such a panacea in these situations, and extra rations of wine and beer were a traditional part of the service. The military brothels were also set up, and Ainley describes the women who worked in them as 'cheerful and hardworking'.[2]

His book also makes it clear that the French ultimately lost the war in Indo-China because of the failure of the régime, both military and civil, to defeat the Vietminh by either outright war or political repression. Both methods were ruthlessly pursued; and Ainley implies that whereas he was sometimes sickened by what he saw, he finally accepted it as a fact of the legionnaire's life.

The justification for such repressive methods as the authorities felt forced to employ in Indo-China was the attempt to crush rebellion, to pacify the colony, and to bring to it the benefits of European culture. Something positive was, of course, achieved: schools and hospitals were built, roads were made, piracy was challenged, trade encouraged. In this, the Legion, as always, was used as a work force. But the covert resistance of the population and the open opposition of the guerillas never flagged. Because of this the winning of skirmishes made no difference, since the losses of the Legion were no longer compensated for by the acquisition of territory or the discouragement of the enemy. The Legion won the battle at Phu Tong Hoa, for instance: that is, a company of the Third Regiment managed to hold on to the fort even though all its officers were killed and half the company put out of action. But the district was no more pacified after the battle than before.

Legionnaires today are trained on Corsica where recruits are given an intensive course in the strategy and techniques of modern warfare.

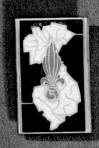

By 1950 the Vietminh resistance had evolved from an underground, guerilla-type movement into a centrally organized administration with a modern army. Its political ideology had not materially changed; nor had its leader, Ho Chi Minh. It was the military position and its leader, a certain Vo Nguyen-Giap, the Vietminh minister of war, that had changed.

General Giap was now in command of a regular army with armour, artillery, and infantry, though without an air force. Because the war took place in dense jungle (the perfect cover for men, material, and foot trails), an air force was not a weapon vital for victory. General Giap was prepared to meet the French in open battle without air support. The French were not prepared to accept the challenge, even with air support. They had learnt their lesson in 1950 at Cao Bang, two hundred miles north-east of Hanoi, where Giap's new army had overrun the line of forts along the Cao Bang ridge, wiped out two complete Legion battalions, pushed relentlessly on towards the Red River and Hanoi itself, decimated the élite parachute troops who were thrown in to halt the retreat, and finally crossed the Red River itself. Cao Bang seemed an omen of what was to come. But the Legion needed no omens.

So the whole picture in Indo-China had changed. The French were now immobilized and the Vietnamese were on the offensive. The French had decided (perforce) on a static war, based on the 'hedgehog' system: that is, strongpoints linked not by roads – there was no time now for the Legion to build roads – but by air. As soon as a fort was attacked, it radioed to headquarters at Hanoi for help. Legion parachutists were then loaded into old Junker transport planes and, hopefully, dropped in the rear of the besieging army. The manoeuvre was not, of course, simple. The mountains and jungles were not precisely mapped; the pilots had to fly 'by guess and by God'; their planes were slow and unreliable; and the paratroopers had to jump into unknown country. But the system seemed to work, for a time. As a result, the French made the momentous decision to defend North Vietnam and Laos by establishing a large fortress in the middle of enemy territory, garrisoning it with an army of élite troops, and supplying it from Hanoi 200 miles to the east by air. This vital strongpoint was Dien Bien Phu.

Regimental badges of the Legion. Most of the badges include the Legion's colours of red and green. The seven-flamed grenade is the oldest of the corp's insignia, but some regiments have preferred designs symbolizing particular campaigns: a map of Indo-China, a Moslem minaret, the Mexican eagle, the Cross of Lorraine.

General Giap, the victor of Dien Bien Phu, was at first thought to be undertaking an impossible task in attempting to reduce the French fortress. The battle cost the French over 46,000 killed, wounded, or captured.

The garrison of Dien Bien Phu consisted of 16,000 men, of whom 4,800 were legionnaires. The number and quality of troops employed in the defence of the camp, the figures for the artillery and the bomber planes (to be used as artillery), and the building of outlying forts to protect the airstrip show how determined the French Command was to use Dien Bien Phu as the anvil on which the army of General Giap was to be smashed. Yet military commentators have, with hindsight, been asking ever since what possessed the French to hole up in this manner?

The answer is that they underestimated General Giap and thought the position impregnable. As General Navarre, French commander-in-chief, explained, the mountain crests which overlooked the camp in the plain below were six to ten miles away, too far for the Vietminh artillery to interdict the air strip on which Dien Bien Phu depended. And even if they attempted to move their guns closer on the slopes of the hills, continued the French general, they would be located by spotter planes and destroyed by powerful artillery.

But General Giap worked patiently and methodically, during the winter months from December 1953 to March 1954, to enclose the French camp in an iron ring of cannon and eight infantry divisions, a total of some 80,000 troops. Giap's strategy now became clear. With his superior manpower and his guns placed on dominating heights which encircled the French army, his final requirement was to interdict the airfield which was the ultimate means of survival for the besieged. However, the French had also taken this into account, and they had fortified three commanding hilltops overlooking the airstrip, one called Gabrielle to the north, one called Beatrice to the north-east, and one called Isabelle to the south. The Legion was responsible for Beatrice and Isabelle, the Algerian Riflemen for Gabrielle. The biggest French guns, the 155 mm. cannon, and what armour was available were also positioned at these outposts. Inside the ring of fortifications, the French had made sure that all was in order for an indefinite siege: hospitals, storehouses, first aid stations, wireless station, dormitories, canteens, even two brothels served by Ouled Nail girls.

But the Vietminh army, largely trained and supplied by the victorious Chinese communists, no longer fought in the traditional oriental manner. Rather than employing massed frontal assaults, General Giap used the tactics of western commanders: the softening up of the objective by prolonged and accurate shelling and the final assault by shock troops relying not on horns and gongs, as in the old wars, but on modern explosives such as plastic charges, Bangalore torpedoes, and bazookas.

In mid-March 1954 he launched his final offensive. In the evening of 13 March the strongpoint Beatrice, which protected the main airstrip and was manned by the Third Battalion of the now-famous Thirteenth Demi-Brigade, was shelled by batteries of guns which included 105 mm. cannon. The shells made direct hits on the fort at the rate of ten every minute, the bombardment continuing for an hour. At the end of that time, the commander of Beatrice, Lieutenant-Colonel Gaucher, had been killed, and scores of legionnaires were either dead or gravely wounded. It must have been made fairly obvious in that fateful hour that Dien Bien Phu was indefensible; and if the fortress's commander, General de Castries, had any doubts, the manner in which Giap's assault troops stormed the battered strongpoint and overwhelmed the garrison must have been the final proof. Not only a vital position but practically an entire battalion of legionnaires had been lost within six hours.

Still the French fought on, though, ominously, the customary grandiose phrases were beginning to be heard by the end of March: 'You will fight to the last man', 'We will never surrender', 'You must hold out', *et cetera*. For the legionnaires, and particularly the newly-formed parachute battalions, there was no need to talk in these terms: they were, as always, expendable. Their job was to counter-attack, regain strongpoints, and prevent the Vietminh from extending the tentacles of their trench system which were now reaching out to the central forts – Anne-Marie, Huguette, Dominique, Françoise, Claudine, and Eliane – to the airstrip, and even towards General de Castries' command post. The paratroopers were ordered again and again to attack and counter-attack wherever the enemy had seized vital positions. By the end of April the enemy had already seized four of the main bastions; the other five were closely invested; the airstrip was inter-dicted and no longer usable; and the vanguard of the Vietminh were within 600 yards of General de Castries' headquarters.

The First Parachute Battalion of the Legion, together with all the other battalions, was now so depleted that they had to be replaced at all costs. Only 100 of the original 700 had survived. And so on 10 April the Second Parachute Battalion was dropped into the 'bowl' (as Dien Bien Phu was aptly described). The Vietminh were waiting for them. (There is little doubt that every move made by the French, particularly in Hanoi, headquarters of General Navarre, was reported to General Giap, not so much by spies as by sympathizers.) Paratroopers were shot as they descended or as soon as they touched down. Others were impaled on coils of barbed wire; others knifed by Viet commandos. The survivors were quickly marshalled together and sent at once to relieve men nearly dead with fatigue in the last remaining outposts of the camp.

There was no change in the situation until, promptly, according to the calendar, the monsoon brought the rains on 20 April. The entire camp was soon inundated and ankle-deep in mud. Life, even during the brief periods of calm, became a nightmare. Even the hospital was half

Dien Bien Phu, defended by nine 'impregnable' forts.

Dien Bien Phu

Gabrielle

Beatrice

N

Anne-Marie

Airstrip

Huguette

Dominique

Françoise

Dien Bien Phu

Claudine

Eliane

Highway 41

Nam Youm

0   1   2   3 Kilometres
0   1   2 Miles

Isabelle

under water, and the appalling conditions under which, in the end, he worked for twenty-four hours a day, are described by Major Paul Grauwin of the Medical Corps, the surgeon who volunteered to serve at Dien Bien Phu.

> At the end of April when the rains came, it was even worse. Water was trickling down everywhere and only evaporating very slowly. The heat became damp and smelly. Blood, vomit, and faeces mixed with the mud made up a frightful compound which stuck to the boots in thick layers.
>
> I shall never forget the martyrdom endured by men wounded in the thorax, trying in vain to get into their lungs the air and oxygen on which their lives depended; and my oxygen cylinders were emptied at a crazy rate. I had to put these patients in the farthest of the Air Commandos' shelters, where the main passage was not covered over ... When I saw them again, a pleural effusion was gently taking them to their death.[3]

Obviously the last days of the fortress and its defenders were near. Only one strongpoint, Isabelle, and the command post complex, which included the camp hospital, remained in French hands. The scenes in this underground charnel house defied description. Dr Grauwin was operating night and day with only an hour's rest in the twenty-four.

> Three days and three nights had gone by. After the last operation I staggered, half-conscious, towards the rectangle of grey light, down there at the end of the passage ... Then I heard a small voice whispering somewhere behind me, 'Oh, I would like to go to sleep and never, never wake up again.' I turned and saw Geneviève, leaning against the wall behind me. She was quietly crying.[4]

Geneviève de Galard-Terraubes was the nurse who survived the destruction by shell fire of the last ambulance plane to land at Dien Bien Phu. She stayed to the end of the siege when she was taken prisoner together with the only other women caught in the trap of the encircled fortress. They were twelve Ouled Nail prostitutes of the military brothel, who had volunteered to work in the hospital during the last few weeks of ceaseless inferno. Every man in the camp was either fighting, dying, or lying helplessly wounded.

The end was near. The Legion, which was largely responsible for the strongpoints with the names of pretty girls (Dominique, Anne-Marie, Françoise, Claudine), was being gradually decimated. The Vietminh never stopped bombarding their redoubts and never stopped digging the trenches which edged every day closer to the command post itself. Here General de Castries must have realized that the end was inevitable.

Neither the Legion nor the paratroopers could save the day. Dien Bien Phu was another Camerone, and everybody now knew it. This must have been in the general's thought as he made his last visit to the main hospital where the seriously wounded now lay in their hundreds, some of them blinded, some with limbs missing, some with head, chest and stomach wounds, at a time when the supplies of drugs, oxygen, saline solutions and antibiotics were all exhausted. In fact, nearly everything and everybody was exhausted. Men were now dying of sheer fatigue. Those who still carried on had become mere automata.

Such were the remnants of the Legion's Thirteenth Demi-Brigade commanded by Colonel André Lalande, the officer who had been with that unit in the raid on Narvik and at Bir Hakeim. These surviving legionnaires had managed to hold on to the strongpoint called Isabelle, the only one of the nine still left in French hands. Every other post had been overrun by thousands upon thousands of Vietminh.

As the forts protecting the perimeter collapsed, the wounded in the field hospitals had been moved to Major Grauwin's main hospital.

Suddenly I saw a long line of muddy statues – but they were moving, groping their way along the walls . . . Under their layers of mud they were quite naked. One of them had a leg missing. How had he managed to get here? Another had an arm missing. Another had only one eye. Then men with plaster on their shoulders, their thorax, their legs. There was mud over everything, dressings and plaster.[5]

It was, of course, the end, and General de Castries was about to surrender; but Colonel Lalande and his 600 remaining legionnaires decided to fight their way out. The idea was to break through the enemy lines to the jungle and to find their way westwards to Laos. Of the 600 only three ever succeeded in getting there. The rest were either killed or driven back to Isabelle, where they finally surrendered.

So ended the Battle of Dien Bien Phu with the surrender of what was left of the garrison. It was one of the most decisive battles of world history during which 10,482 legionnaires had been killed, over 30,000 wounded, and 6,328 captured – an average loss of just under 6,000 highly-trained professional soldiers a year. They, together with the élite of the French officer corps, seemed to have died in vain, for not only had Indo-China been lost, but the very forces, political as well as military, which had made the conquest of that Far Eastern colony possible had been wholly discredited. The French Empire in Asia was ended.

Algeria 1954-62

The obvious lesson of Indo-China was that nationalist rebellions could no longer be crushed by military force. But the French government, the army, and the majority of the people regarded the defeat in Vietnam, like the defeat in France in 1940, as a matter of national honour. There was, therefore, no hesitation about again attempting to crush rebellion, this time in Algeria; and there was no difficulty in recruiting men for the Legion which was expected to do it.

In fact, by 1954, when Indo-China was lost and its presence was needed in Algeria, the Legion had become an army in itself: it now consisted of some 36,000 men. The regular troops which the French brought into Algeria during the revolt eventually amounted to another 350,000, most of them conscripts used for policing the rear areas. Nearly all the front-line fighting was left to the Legion.

But the war that was to convulse Algeria and, for that matter, France itself, for the next eight years was the kind of war in which one side has an enormous army equipped with every possible military device and the other side has no army at all and no weapons other than what a man can carry. Hence there were to be no large-scale battles, no great victories or defeats.

The rebels (as the dissident Algerians were regarded by the French) were not organized into a recognizable army, but operated in small units throughout the whole of the country, with the exception of the Saharan oases in the south. This region remained comparatively quiet while resistance to the French occupation took the form of killings and bombings in the cities and towns of the north. In so far as the revolt was a political movement, it was directed by the self-appointed leaders of the *Front National de Libération* (the F.L.N.). These men, who were constantly being sought out by the French security forces, moved about the country with their supporters terrorizing in particular small settlements, such as villages and farms, and often killing native Algerians suspected of being sympathetic to the French. In the large cities the

Legion paratroopers found themselves at the barricades facing right-wing territorials who were prepared to fight to keep Algeria French.

F.L.N. succeeded in organizing bombings, terrorism, and general strikes to the extent of bringing normal life to a standstill, as they did in the capital, Algiers, for instance. The bombings, as always, were the greatest menace, since no one knew where they would occur or whom they would kill. Moreover, it was impossible to identify the bombers who included students and girls as well as trained saboteurs and ex-criminals. And in the beginning of this reign of terrorism, the rebel leaders had a sanctuary in the Casbah, the famous native quarter of Algiers, where they set up something of a government in exile, with committees of action, of propaganda, and even of taxation by means of which they collected £100,000 a month from the local population. Once these squads started exploding bombs in the European parts of the city, choosing crowded cafés and restaurants, the character of the war between the French and the nationalists changed. For the effect of the bombs, the terrorism, and the general strikes was almost equivalent to a major battlefield victory for the F.L.N.

The problem of the security forces, therefore, was to root out the bombers and, in particular, their leaders. The paratroopers did so in precisely six months by the simple expedient of sealing off the Casbah, patrolling the alleys night and day, keeping in touch with headquarters by walkie-talkie telephones, raiding suspect houses, paying for information, and torturing known members of the F.L.N. Besides this, taking a leaf out of the book of authoritarian governments, the paratroopers introduced the 'block system' whereby one person was held responsible for the activities and even the whereabouts of several others, family and neighbours.

But the activities of the F.L.N. were not confined to the major cities. In the field, the Legion had a vast area to police – 847,500 square miles forming a colony four times as large as France itself. The two contingent nations, Tunisia to the east and Morocco to the west, both independent countries since March 1956, were strong allies of the F.L.N. and were openly used as sanctuaries by these fighters. In order to seal off the two frontiers and to prevent squads of rebels trained in Tunisia and Morocco from crossing into Algeria, the French had built two so-called barrages

(*right*) The brunt of the fighting in Algeria was left to the Legion. There were few pitched battles, however, as the F.L.N. relied on terrorist activities both in the cities and the surrounding countryside. Algerians considered loyal to the French were murdered and their homes and farms burnt.

consisting of electrified fences (charged with 5,000 volts at night), mine-fields, searchlights, and machine-gun posts, continuously patrolled by motorized cavalry units. The eastern barrage ran from the Mediter-ranean to Négrine just west of Gafsa and north of the salt lake called Chott Djerid; the western barrage from the Mediterranean to Colomb-Béchar. On the whole the system worked.

But the F.L.N. at no time depended on a regular army. It called itself a guerilla movement and fought with guerilla tactics. The guerilla unit, called a *khatiba*, was seldom more than one hundred men strong and therefore no match for even a single company of legionnaires. Indeed, when a Legion company managed to engage an F.L.N. *khatiba*, there was never any doubt about the outcome. Aware of this, the Algerians with-drew to the mountains and fought a rearguard action from crest to crest, cave to cave, and even boulder to boulder. If the Legion felt they had cornered their adversary, they called in their strike planes to fire rockets and machine-guns into the insurgents' hideout. It was that kind of skirmishing all over Algeria, especially in the mountains; and it was that kind of indecisive war for some eight years.

In fact, from the Legion's point of view, the war had come to consist of only two sorts of action: *quadrillage*, or search operations based on a pattern of squares; and *ratissage* (literally 'raking') or cleaning up an area by arrests and threats of reprisals. The more ineffective the *quad-rillage* and *ratissage*, the more severe were the methods used to quell the insurrection. Under the name of 'pacification', for instance, the civilian authorities removed a million Moslems from their villages and placed them in special camps supervised by the military. Such methods, reminiscent of the Nazi concentration camps, were condemned by the outside world, so that whereas the generals, by one means or another, had actually crushed practically all overt military resistance throughout the country, the politicians had increased the underground hostility a hundredfold.

The Legion – particularly the *para* units – had, in their determination to win this particular fight, also contributed to the ultimate victory of the Algerian freedom-fighters. As with all professional soldiers fighting guerillas, the army resorted in the end to extracting information by torture, summary arrests and trials of civilians, executions, and concen-tration camps. The F.L.N. guerillas replied by publicizing these activities to the outside world in such first-hand accounts as Henri Alleg's *La Question*. There was no doubt now that the French, who had won a military victory in Algeria, had lost the peace and with it their largest and richest colony; for their own people were now disillusioned, disillusioned not only with a half-a-dozen governments at home, seven successive generals in Algeria, and twenty years of continual war in Europe, the Far East, and now Africa, but with the whole concept of nineteenth-century colonialism itself. Their dilemma was to extricate themselves from Algeria by avoiding an outright defeat on the scale of the Indo-Chinese campaign; and for this they looked for a father-figure, a known patriot, and a statesman of unblemished reputation. They found such a saviour in General Charles de Gaulle.

But all this talk of compromise, of peace, and of independence was one thing to the civilians at home, but something entirely different to the Algerian colonists on the one hand and the Foreign Legion on the other. Both these groups had this much in common: both had really created modern Algeria and Algeria was now their country – *Algérie française*, as they called it. They were determined, therefore, not to relinquish their homeland without a struggle.

The rest of the story belongs more to political than to military history, though there was a brief moment when the latter became the more important. On 21 April 1961 the Legion's First Paratroop Regiment joined a military coup aimed at keeping Algeria French and prepared to defy General de Gaulle himself. The leader of this army revolt was none other than General Maurice Challe, commander-in-chief, a soldier-aviator of extreme right-wing tendencies, placed 'under surveillance' in 1958, and reinstated by General de Gaulle in 1959. General Challe was supported by some 8,000 French troops, most of them paratroopers, including legionnaires and, of course, by the right-wing colonists. These men were to form the notorious O.A.S. (*Organisation de l'Armée Sécrète*) which was to fight to the end to keep Algeria French and was to use assassination as one of its weapons.

But the military coup was abortive, for, unexpectedly as it happened, the Legion did not support it. Even more important, neither did the Air Force, nor the Navy. The insurrectionists had particularly hoped for the collaboration of the former as there was talk of a parachute mission on France! But the French pilots either flew their planes empty back to France, or refused to take them off the ground. The navy replied by opening fire on a parachute battalion which marched on Mers-el-Kebir. That was the end of the plotters' hopes and expectations. General Challe surrendered. The dissident troops were simply marched off to detention camps. The French had suffered what they called, with reason, 'a diplomatic Dien Bien Phu'.

The revolt of the First Paratroop Regiment against the French government was a blow to the Legion's prestige. Once again some French people became wary of a body of foreign mercenaries who might at any time threaten the security of the state.

Moreover, the Legion – the old Legion of men with long bayonets, men who could march thirty miles in a night and fight at daybreak – was not needed in quite the same way as it had been in Mexico, Madagascar, Dahomey, the Sahara, Morocco, and Indo-China: needed, that is, to conquer and police a huge empire. That empire no longer existed; Algeria had achieved independence. The original *raison d'être* of the Legion seemed, at the time, to have gone.

The end of a whole era was symbolized in a ceremony conducted on 29 September 1962. On that day General Jacques Lefort, the newly-appointed Inspector General of the Legion, officially closed the Hall of Honour and the Monument to the Dead at Sidi-bel-Abbès. In a short ceremony, the famous banners and standards were taken down, the reliquaries containing the wooden hand of Captain Danjou and the ashes of the American legionnaire, William Moll, were removed, and the coffins containing the mortal remains of General Rollet, 'the father of the Legion', of Prince Aage, and of the unknown legionnaire were disinterred. They were then flown in a special aeroplane from Sidi-bel-Abbès to an airfield near Aubagne, the new headquarters of the Legion. The banners, standards, and sacred relics were re-dedicated and set up in a new Hall of Fame; the bodies of the dead heroes were re-interred in a new Legion cemetery in the nearby village of Puyloubier.

But the new home of the Legion cannot altogether evoke the *mystique* of the Quartier Vienot, the main barracks at Sidi-bel-Abbès. For, with its battle flags, decorations, relics, and mementoes of every colonel of the regiment amassed over almost one hundred years, the Quartier Vienot was more like a cathedral than a barracks. Indeed, the Hall of Honour, the Monument to the Dead, and the Legion Cemetery had, certainly for the legionnaires themselves, the same mystery that the altar and tombs of a church have for a devout Christian. For therein was enshrined a long history of unparalleled courage symbolized in the sacred objects – all manifestations of a special cult which has always made the Legion quite separate from regular military units and explains the motto *Legio Patria Nostra*.

An emotional scene at the end of the Algerian war as rebel Legion paratroopers are disarmed, ordered from their camp, and sent to an undisclosed destination. A woman sympathizer blows kisses as they leave.

Epilogue

With the end of the Algerian War of Independence, the Legion may have fought its last major battle in defence of the French empire which it had played a leading role in creating. The present force, now dispersed in small detachments in the Mediterranean, Africa, the Pacific, and elsewhere, is unlikely to be called upon to suppress uprisings on the scale of those of Indo-China or Algeria. But this has not altered the Legion's attitude to its special constitution and function. It continues to accept suitable volunteers in the customary manner; to train them according to the traditional methods; to provide garrison troops for remote outposts; to use such troops for road-building and construction works; and, above all, to uphold the unique traditions of the corps.

Yet the legionnaires at present on active service do not think of their regiments in terms of '*la légion de papa*' or 'Dad's Army'. On the contrary, they are resentful of the vague generalized view that they are now picturesque, ceremonial soldiers in the same class as the Vatican's Swiss Guards or the Tower of London Beefeaters. In fact, one has the impression in talking to serving officers and men that the weighty tradition deriving from Camerone can be something of a liability, since the cult of the final desperate bayonet charge, so characteristic of the nineteenth-century battles, has little relevance to the grim realities of modern warfare. Indeed, a visit to Legion detachments today leaves the observer with the impression that there are, in a sense, two legions: the legion of history (at Aubagne and Puyloubier) and the Legion of the future on Corsica and in the garrison outposts in Africa and French Oceania. Yet both combine to make one and the same élite corps.

The observer is bound to ask, what *is* the future and what the function of this unique corps? Part of the answer can be given at once. In the event of hostilities involving France, the Legion would certainly be rushed to the centre of the trouble where it would, just as certainly, conduct itself as it has always done, with valour beyond the call of duty. For one must always remember a basic fact about the Foreign Legion:

Legion headquarters, no longer at famed Sidi-bel-Abbès, are now at Aubagne, Marseilles. But the spirit, or *mystique*, of the Legion is unchanged.

it is made up for the most part of men for whom war is not merely a career, but a vocation.

It follows that as long as there are wars or threats of war, such a force is an invaluable asset to the French military establishment. But it is, or could be, more than that. It could in certain circumstances be deployed as a military police force, and one cannot think of any more effective unit than the Foreign Legion in those cases where the United Nations undertakes to patrol areas of conflict. The Legion has two exceptional qualifications for such a job: first, it is a genuine international force whose loyalty is to itself and not to a foreign power; and second, it is certain not to have problems of discipline. Even so, the use of the Legion as an international police force is, at present, an academic question, with political overtones which cannot be discussed here.

In the meantime, the Legion continues to be ready for all contingencies in a new era of warfare in which it recognizes that the bayonet is as obsolete as the crossbow. At the same time, it remains firmly tied to certain concepts, attitudes, and traditions which have always distinguished it from other famous regiments. One cannot, indeed, escape the impression that it belongs in spirit to those brotherhoods associated with the medieval knights. There is no mistaking this aspect of fraternity when one sees the extent of its international network of associations, societies, and clubs vaguely reminiscent of certain religious orders. In short, once a legionnaire always a legionnaire, and as with any order which practises as well as preaches brotherhood, a member will never be abandoned, whatever his misfortunes. The proof of this is seen in the Provençal village of Puyloubier where the Legion has its *Institution des Invalides* and its own cemetery. Here, in a private domain, live some hundred *pensionnaires*, old soldiers with war wounds, others with economic, social, or personal problems, others learning a craft in order to be rehabilitated into the outside world. All are granted the free, generous, and unquestioning aid of the *Service du Morale*. At Auriol a *Maison de Retraite* is set aside for those *anciens combattants* who elect to end their lives inside the confines and in the care of the Legion. It is, then, a manifestation of the Legion's *mystique* to visit Auriol and Puyloubier and see the old soldiers wandering about in the grounds of their chateau, undergoing treatment for their disabilities, working in the handicraft centres, or simply resting until they wish to return to the world which, for a time, they feel unable to cope with.

It is this non-institutional type of charity which helps to explain the loyalty of those ex-legionnaires who survived the ordeals first of the

ECPA

The Foreign Legion, like their Roman predecessors in Africa, the Third Augusta, were builders as well as soldiers. Road construction was their *forte*.

règlement itself, then of the campaigns in which they have fought over the last thirty years. It explains, too, the loyalty of those now ageing men who belong to associations of former legionnaires all over the world, men who are now businessmen, civil servants, head waiters, taxi-drivers, telephone operators, and so forth, but who are a little different as a result of their experiences.

It explains why one of them can write:

The Legion is (and was) the most honourable place in the world for those who do not want to make compromises. The Legion was the only place in the world where no one has ever lied to me, where I was treated with absolute respect as a man.[1]

and why an Englishman, who admittedly only joined for adventure, sums up his experience like this:

If you found a fault in the Legion, it was a fault in yourself. The Legion did not ask or force you, it was your own free will. *Nobody asked you to join.* In the end, the Legion made me look at men for what they were and not the race they came from; and though it may sound strange, what I did learn was compassion.[2]

Strange, indeed, since many legionnaires will admit that soon after they enlisted they either tried to desert or entertained ideas of deserting because of the severity of the discipline and training. Obviously the severity was such that in the end a man could only accept it if he accepted the code on which it was based: first, that the 'good' soldier is one who has been trained and conditioned to die, if necessary, without reservations; and secondly, that his first loyalty is to his regiment. This being so, it is obvious that the quality and character of the officers commanding him are of prime importance, so it is not surprising that the French High Command, once the special value of the Legion was recognized, has always breveted the cream of the military academies to the officer corps of the Legion. The majority of these officers were, in the nature of French military tradition, strongly royalist, ultra-conservative, and rigidly Catholic – 'approachable in a way that a seigneur is approachable to his peasantry'.[3] Yet, almost without exception, they were deeply concerned with their men's welfare; and without exception, they led their legionnaires into battle with a special and sometimes even eccentric style of their own.

Indeed, it is this relationship which is essential to the mental and moral wellbeing of the legionnaire, who has few other compensations for the sacrifice of his freedom. He knows that when he enlists, he has in effect signed away his nationality and placed himself outside the protection of his country's government. Thenceforward, he can only look to the Legion for help and hope, and if he is prepared to accept the inviolable rules, he will rarely look in vain. *Legio patria nostra* is not merely a motto. It is a statement of fact; and it explains why some ex-legionnaires never really leave this homeland at all.

Such a man was 'Big' Nichols who had been an officer in the United States Army during the First World War. He had been decorated by the French Government with the *Légion d'Honneur* for an act of bravery involving a blazing ammunition ship at Marseilles. After the war, he had joined the Legion and had remained in it until his early sixties. He was permitted to sign on for only a year at a time, and it was an annual ordeal to go before the Commandant and plead for permission to engage for one more year's service. By this time, of course, he was a pure supernumerary, and his nominal duty was to play the tuba in the Legion's band (*la musique*). But he seemed to please himself whether he paraded or not, and as a result the band was often minus one tuba-player and one tuba. He was almost permanently drunk and had adopted the annoying habit of sauntering past the guard-room, his *Légion d'Honneur* dangling provocatively at the end of its crimson ribbon. The guard was obliged to present arms to a chevalier of the Legion of Honour, but Legionnaire Second Class Nichols was well and truly cursed for all that. In other words, he was a nuisance, a lost soul, who had no other home than the Legion where he spent two months out of every year in hospital recovering from dipsomania. When he died eventually in an aura of alcohol, the Legion buried him with full military honours.[4]

Even today, the Legion is ready to take care of its own. Burial in the cemetery at Puyloubier is arranged for those who request it, and here they are interred near the great wall inscribed with the names of those who died in colonial wars all over the world. General Rollet, the 'Father of the Legion' and Prince Aage of Denmark lie here among the serried rows of legionnaires with exotic and unpronounceable names.

The museum at Aubagne, too, symbolizes the quasi-religious *mystique*, with exhibits like 'the cross and a fragment of bone found in the tomb of Second Lieutenant Maudet, who died of wounds received at Camerone'. Another exhibit is the tunic of Captain Danjou himself, 'presented by the nephew of the hero'. On the wall hangs the *Médaille Militaire* of Alan Seeger and the citation that went with it:

Jeune légionnaire, enthousiaste et énergétique, aimant passionnément la France, engagé volontairement au début des hostilités et faisant preuve d'un courage et d'entrain admirables, glorieusement tombé le 11 juillet 1916 devant Belloy-en-Santerre.

à Bel-Abbès, 24 juillet 1924
le colonel Boulet-Desbareau
commandant le 4ème Régiment Etranger

(This young, enthusiastic and energetic legionnaire, who loved France deeply, enlisted voluntarily at the beginning of the hostilities and gave proof of admirable courage and enterprise. He fell gloriously on 11 July 1916 in front of Belloy-en-Santerre. Sidi-bel-Abbès, 24 July 1924. Colonel Boulet-Desbareau, commanding the 4th Legion Regiment.)

And so one comes away from the Legion's headquarters with its barracks, museum, homes, hospitals, and cemetery for those who have passed on with an impression of separateness that one finds in monasteries. This feeling has nothing to do with the distinctive uniform – the white kepi and red and green epaulettes, or such differences from the usual military practices as the Legion's style of marching (80 to 85 paces a minute as compared with the regular army's 110 to 115) or the bizarre marching hymn, *Le Boudin*:

> *Tiens! Voilà du boudin, voilà du boudin, voilà du boudin.*
> *Pour les Alsaciens, les Suisses et les Lorrains.*
> *Pour les Belges y en a plus, pour les Belges y en a plus.*
> *Ce sont des tireurs au cul.*
>
> *(Look! There is the black pudding . . .*
> *For the Alsatians, the Swiss and the Lorrains.*
> *For the Belgians there is none . . .*
> *The Belgians are lousy shots!)*

The *mystique* derives, one feels, from an unquestioning belief in the kind of creed by which the warrior class has always lived from the time of the Persian Immortals. It is the mentality of the legionnaire that matters – not what uniform he wears today, as parachutist, skier, commando, or frogman, even though such specialization seems to make him a totally different animal from the high-casqued, musket-armed, spade-toting legionnaire of the 1830s. These differences in appearance do not signify. Nor for that matter do the decisions of politicians, the efforts of statesmen to maintain the balance of power, or the new lethal weapons of the scientists. The Legion remains fundamentally unchanged, and will undoubtedly remain so until it is abolished altogether. For the legionnaire himself has no country and no home other than his regiment for the duration of his service, whether he is a king like Peter the First of Serbia, a prince like Aage of Denmark, a pretender to a throne like the Count of Paris, a poet like Blaise Cendrars, or a man without any legal identity at all. He is a legionnaire.

The tombs of Legionnaire Zimmerman, Captain Aage, and General Rollet before the cenotaph, in the cemetery at Puyloubier, which honours the Legion's dead.

Bibliographical Notes

Chapter 1

1 Evidence of this reticence is seen in the official military histories, such as General Paul Azan's *Conquête et Pacification de l'Algérie* (Paris: Villain et Bar 1931) in which the Legion's existence and its exploits are scarcely mentioned. It was not even included in the *Army List of Regiments* until 1931.

2 George Manington *A Soldier of the Legion* (London: Murray 1907) pp. 9–11.

3 Ibid pp. 39–40.

4 Christian A. R. Aage, Prince of Denmark *My Life in the Foreign Legion* (London: Nash and Grayson 1928).

5 Alan Seeger *Poems*. With an introduction by William Archer (London: Constable; New York: AMS Press, 1917) p. 144.

6 Count P. de Castellane *Military Life in Algiers* (London: Hurst and Blackett 1853) vol. 1 pp. 237–8.

7 Ernst F. Löhndorff *Hell in the Foreign Legion*. Translated by Gerard Shelley. (London: Allen and Unwin 1931) p. 137.

8 Michael Donovan *March or Die!* (London: Cassell 1932) p. 81.

9 *Ibid* p. 84.

10 Löhndorff, op. cit. p. 244.

11 A. R. Cooper *The Man Who Liked Hell* (London: Jarrolds 1933) p. 9.

12 Major Zinovi Pechkoff *The Bugle Sounds. Life in the Foreign Legion* (London and New York: Appleton 1926) p. 78.

13 Aage, op. cit. p. 8.

Chapter 2

1 Le Capitaine M.S.J.A. Blanc *La Légion Etrangère* (Paris: Blanpain 1890) pp. 17–18.

2 Camille Félix Michel Rousset *Les commencements d'une conquête d'Algérie de 1830–1840* (Paris: Librarie Plon 1887) p. 81.

3 Translated by the author from an article by Count G. de Villebois Mareuil 'La Légion Etrangère' in *Revue des Deux Mondes* vol. 134 1896, p. 876.

4 See G. M. *La Légion Etrangère et les Troupes Coloniales* (Paris: R. Chapelot 1903) p. 9.

Chapter 3

1 See James Wellard *The Great Sahara* (London: Hutchinson; New York: Dutton, 1965) chapters 3 and 4.

Chapter 5

1 See L. Vandevelde *Précis historique et critique de la Campagne d'Italie en 1859* (Paris: Tanera 1860).

Chapter 6

1 For the early exploration of the Sahara by civilians, see James Wellard *The Great Sahara* chapter 7.

2 Sir Richard Burton *A Mission to Gelele, King of Dahome*, edited by C. W. Newbury (London: Routledge and Kegan Paul; New York: Praeger, 1966) p. 262.

3 Ibid pp. 261–2.

4 Ibid p. 264.

5 Ibid pp. 284, 285.

6 Jules Poirier *Campagne du Dahomey* (Paris et Limoges: Charles Lavauzelle 1895) p. 3.

7 Kathleen Shervinton *The Shervintons, Soldiers of Fortune* (London: Unwin 1899) pp. 96–7.

8 Poirier, op. cit. p. 252.

Chapter 7

1 Marcel Poulin *L'Amiral Courbet, sa jeunesse, sa vie militaire et sa mort* (Limoges: Ardant 1888) p. 67.

2 Manington, op. cit. pp. 51–4.

3 Ibid p. 164.

4 Commandant Charles Hubert *Le Colonel Dominé* (Paris: Editions Berger-Levrault 1938) p. 66.

5 Ibid p. 93.

6 Ibid p. 255.

Chapter 8

1 From M.-C. Poinsot *Les Volontaires Etrangers de 1914* (Paris: Dorbon-Aine 1915) p. 31–2. Translation by the author.

2 Ibid p. 32.

3 Ibid pp. 38–41.

4 Alan Seeger *Poems* (London: Constable; New York: AMS Press 1917) p. 173.

Chapter 9

1 Ex-Legionnaire 75,645 *Slaves of Morocco* (London: Sampson Low 1938) pp. 144–6.

2 Christian A. R. Aage *My Life in the Foreign Legion* (London: Nash and Grayson 1928) pp. 102–3.

3 Ex-Legionnaire 1,384 *Hell Hounds of France* (London: Sampson Low 1932) pp. 8–9.

4 For an account of this, see Ex-legionnaire 75,645, op. cit., although a great deal of

this book reads more like cheap fiction than fact.

5 Jean Martin *Je suis un légionnaire* (Paris: Librairie Fayard 1938) pp. 104–5.
6 *Livre d'Or de la Légion Etrangère, 1831–1931* (Limoges: Frazier Soye 1931) p. 272.
7 Ibid p. 284.

Chapter 10
1 Georges Blond *La Légion Etrangère* (Paris: Stock 1964) p. 304.

Chapter 11
1 Henry Ainley *In Order to Die* (London: Burke 1955) p. 14.
2 *Ibid* p. 30.
3 Major Paul Grauwin *Doctor at Dienbienphu* (London: Hutchinson 1955) p. 169.

4 Ibid p. 156.
5 Ibid p. 278.

Epilogue
1 Extract from a letter to the author from Georges Gebhardt, a *caporal-chef* who was a surgeon's mate in the Legion's Airborne Medical Company in Vietnam.
2 From a letter written by E. W. Morgan, who served as a legionnaire *première classe* for five years in Indo-China, Morocco, Algeria, and Tunisia.
3 From ex-legionnaire John Yeowell's manuscript diary of his service in the Legion. Mr Yeowell is Honorary Secretary of the Foreign Legion Association of Great Britain.
4 A story recounted by John Yeowell in the unpublished memoirs of his Legion service and reproduced by permission.

Bibliography

The first section of this bibliography has been selected for those readers who are interested in the historical background against which the Legion waged its campaigns as well as the campaigns themselves.

The second section lists a typical assortment of memoirs both in praise and in condemnation of the Legion. Books referring to particular events will be found in the Bibliographical notes.

General Histories
Azan, General Paul *Conquête et Pacification de l'Algérie*. Les armées françaises d'outre-mer. Série 1, No 1. Paris: Villain et Bar 1931.
Azan, General Paul *La Légion Etrangère en Espagne, 1835–1839*. Paris: Charles Lavauzelle 1907.
Bernelle, General Joseph Nicolas *Histoire de l'ancienne Légion Etrangère : Opérations en 1831, 1832–1835*. Paris: Marc-Aurel 1850.
Blanc, Michel Sylvestre Jacques Alphonse *La Légion Etrangère*. Paris: Blanpain 1890.
Blond, Georges *La Légion Etrangère*. Paris: Stock 1964.
Choulot, Count Paul de *L'Histoire du Premier Régiment de la Légion Etrangère*. Bourges: Just-Bernard 1864.
Grisot, General Paul Adolphe *La Légion Etrangère de 1831–1837*. Paris: Berget-Levrault 1888.
Livre d'Or de la Légion Etrangère, 1831–1931 and *1958*. Paris: Frazier Soye 1931; Limoges: Charles Lavauzelle 1958.
Mercer, Charles Edward *The Foreign Legion*. The History of a Unique Military Tradition. London: New English Library 1966.
Moch, Gaston *La Question de la Légion Etrangère*. Paris: Fasquelle 1914.
Morel, Paul Emile Gustave *La Légion Etrangère*. Paris: Chapelot 1912.
O'Ballance, Edgar *The Story of the French Foreign Legion*. London: Faber 1961.
Perret, Eduouard *Les Français en Afrique. Recits Algériens . . . 1830–1848*. Two vols. Paris: Blond et Barral 1886–1887.
Poirmeur, Marie Emile Henri *Notre Vieille Légion*. Paris: Berger-Levrault 1931.
Rockwell, Paul A. *American Fighters in the Foreign Legion*. Boston: Houghton Mifflin 1930.
Saint-Arnaud, Marshall Eduouard Joseph *Mission . . . aux Confins Sahariens. Etude d'Organization Militaire*. Paris: Michel-Lévy 1908.
Turnbull, Patrick Edward Xenophon *The Foreign Legion*. London: Heinemann 1964.
Vallières, Jean des *Et Voici La Légion Etrangère*. Paris: Bonne 1962.

Villebois-Mareuil, Count Georges de 'La Légion Etrangère', *Revue des deux Mondes*, vol. 134, 1896. pp. 876 ff.

Personal Accounts
Aage, Christian, Prince of Denmark *My Life in the Foreign Legion*. London: Nash and Grayson 1928.
Ainley, Henry *In Order to Die*. London: Burke 1955.
Castellane-Novejan, Count Louis Charles Pierre de *Souvenirs Militaires de l'Algérie*. Translated by Margaret J. Lovett. Two vols. London: Remington 1886.
Chapman, Victor E. *Letters from France*. New York: Macmillan 1917.
Cooper, A. R. *The Man Who Liked Hell: Twelve Years in the French Foreign Legion*. London: Jarrolds 1933.
Cranton, V. *Keepers of the Desert*. London: Sampson Low 1939.
Delmayne, Anthony *Sahara Desert Escape*. London: Jarrolds 1958.
Donovan, Michael *March or Die! An Account of the Author's Experiences in the Foreign Legion*. London: Cassell 1932.
Doty, B. J. *The Legion of the Damned*. London: Cape 1928.
Duplessis, Theodore *Souvenirs de mes Campagnes à la Légion Etrangère en Mexique et Afrique*. Geneva: Jullien 1923.
Ex-Legionnaire 1,384 *Hell Hounds of France*. London: Sampson Low 1932.
Ex-Legionnaire 75,645 *Slaves of Morocco*. London: Sampson Low 1938.
Grauwin, Major Paul *Doctor at Dienbienphu*. Translated by James Oliver. New York: John Day 1955.
Hubert, Charles *Le Colonel Dominé*. Paris: Berger-Levrault 1938.
Legionnaire 17,889 *In the Foreign Legion*. London: Arnold 1915.
Löhndorff, E. F. *Hell in the Foreign Legion*. Translated by Gerard Shelley. London: Allen and Unwin 1931.
Magnus, Maurice *Memoirs of the Foreign Legion*. With a Preface by D. H. Lawrence. London: Secker 1924.
Maire, François Marie *Souvenirs de la Légion Etrangère*. Paris: Michel 1939.
Martyn, Frederic *Life in the Foreign Legion from a Soldier's Point of View*. London: Everett's Library 1911.
Pechkoff, Zinovi *The Bugle Sounds. Life in the Foreign Legion*. London and New York: Appleton 1926.
Price, George Ward *In Morocco with the Legion*. London: Jarrolds 1934.
Seeger, Alan *Letters and Diary*. London: Constable; New York: AMS Press (reprint), 1917.
Sheean, Vincent James *Personal History*. New York: Doubleday 1934.

Illustration Acknowledgments

Figures in **bold type** denote colour illustrations.
The following abbreviations have been used:

BM   British Museum, London (Department of Printed Books)
ECPA Etablissement Cinématographique et Photographique des Armées
IWM Imperial War Museum, London
MA   Collections du Musée de l'Armée, Paris
RT   Radio Times Hulton Picture Library
V&A Victoria and Albert Museum, London

Maps and plans by Tom Stalker-Miller on pages 30, 38, 52, 68, 75, 80, 90, 101, 102, 117

Endpapers From *Conquête et Pacification de l'Algérie* by General Paul Azan 1931. ECPA
Title page 'Corps des Dromadaires, Algérie (1894)' from *Tenues des Troupes de France* Vol. 4, by 'JOB' 1903. V&A.
7   Collection John Kobal
8   ECPA
10–11 From a sketch book by R. Lemmy 1907–60. V&A
13   Associated Press
16   From *In Morocco with the Legion* by G. Ward Price 1934

Index